AQA | AS | UNIT 2

Sociology

Education and Sociological Methods

Emma Jones and Marsha Jones

Series Editor: Joan Garrod

For Lola and Rosie

Philip Allan Updates, an imprint of Hodder Education, part of Hachette UK, Market Place, Deddington, Oxfordshire, OX15 0SE

Orders

Bookpoint Ltd, 130 Milton Park, Abingdon, Oxfordshire, OX14 4SB
tel: 01235 827720
fax: 01235 400454
e-mail: uk.orders@bookpoint.co.uk
Lines are open 9.00 a.m.–5.00 p.m., Monday to Saturday, with a 24-hour message answering service. You can also order through the Philip Allan Updates website: www.philipallan.co.uk

© Philip Allan Updates 2008

ISBN 978-0-340-95806-3

First printed 2008
Impression number 5 4 3 2
Year 2013 2012 2011 2010 2009

This Guide has been written specifically to support students preparing for the AQA AS Sociology Unit 2 examination. The content has been neither approved nor endorsed by AQA and remains the sole responsibility of the authors.

Typeset by Phoenix Photosetting, Chatham, Kent
Printed by MPG Books, Bodmin

Hachette UK's policy is to use papers that are natural, renewable and recyclable products and made from wood grown in sustainable forests. The logging and manufacturing processes are expected to conform to the environmental regulations of the country of origin.

Contents

Introduction

■ ■ ■

Content Guidance

■ ■ ■

Questions and Answers

Introduction

About this guide

This guide is for students following the AQA AS Sociology course. It deals with the Module 2 topic **Education**, which is examined within Unit 2. Although it provides an overview of the main areas within the topic, you should also make sure that you are familiar with the subject matter as given by your teachers.

There are three sections to this guide:

- **Introduction** — this provides advice on how to use this unit guide, guidance on revision and an outline of the assessment aims of AS Sociology. It concludes with guidance on how to succeed in the unit test.
- **Content Guidance** — this provides details of the specification subsections of Education and Sociological Methods. The exam questions on Education can be based on any aspect within the specification, so do not leave out any areas in your revision. Each topic area examines **key ideas**, stating the main points of evaluation and listing the **key concepts** and **key thinkers**.
- **Questions and Answers** — this shows you the kind of questions you can expect in the unit test. The first three question papers are each followed by two sample answers (a C-grade and an A-grade response). These are interspersed with examiner comments so that you can see how the marks are allocated. The fourth question paper is for you to attempt yourself.

How to use the guide

To use this guide to your best advantage, you should refer to the Introduction and Content Guidance sections from the beginning of your study of Education and Sociological Methods. However, in order to get full advantage from the Question and Answer section, you would be advised to wait until you have completed your study of these topics, as the questions are wide-ranging. When you are ready to use this section, you should take each question in turn, study it carefully, and write a full answer. When you have done this, study the grade A candidate's answer and compare it with your own, paying close attention to the examiner's comments. You should also look at the grade C answers and, using the examiner's comments as a guide, work out how to rewrite your answers in order to gain higher marks.

These tasks are quite intensive and time-consuming, and you should not be tempted to try to tackle all the questions in a short space of time. It is better to focus on one at a time, and spread the workload over several weeks. You should be able to find time to do this, even while studying other topics. In addition to using the questions to consolidate your own knowledge and develop your exam skills, you should use at least some of the questions as revision practice — even just reading through the grade A candidate's answers should provide you with useful revision material.

The AS specification

The aims of the AS Sociology course are to enable you to:
- acquire knowledge and a critical understanding of contemporary social processes and social changes
- appreciate the significance of theoretical and conceptual issues in sociological debate
- understand and evaluate sociological methodology and a range of research methods through active involvement in the research process
- develop skills that enable you to focus on personal identity, roles and responsibilities within society
- develop a lifelong interest in social issues

You should be able to focus on contemporary society.

Examinable skills

Assessment objectives 1 and 2 (AO1 and AO2) are an integral part of the AS specification, and each counts for approximately half of the available marks.

Assessment objective 1 (AO1): knowledge and understanding

Knowledge and understanding are linked, therefore you must not only demonstrate possession of sociological knowledge but also be able to use it in a meaningful way. Understanding implies that you can select appropriate knowledge and use it in answer to a specific question. Knowledge and understanding includes the nature of sociological thought, methods of sociological enquiry and two core themes.

The nature of sociological thought
Candidates are required to study the following concepts and theoretical issues:
- social order, social control
- social change
- conflict and consensus
- social structure and social action
- the role of values
- the relationship between sociology and contemporary social policy

Methods of sociological enquiry
Candidates will demonstrate that they are familiar with a range of methods and sources of data, together with an understanding of the relationship between theory and methods, particularly the way sociologists deal with:
- the collection of primary and secondary data
- the analysis of quantitative and qualitative data using appropriate concepts
- the factors influencing the design and conduct of sociological research
- practical, ethical and theoretical issues arising in sociological research

Themes

AS candidates are also required to study two core themes:

- socialisation, culture and identity
- social differentiation, power and stratification

These themes are to be applied to the topic areas in the specification and not tested as separate topics. You will see how these two core themes can be applied to the topic of Education as you read this guide.

Assessment objective 2 (AO2): application, analysis, interpretation and evaluation

The skills that are examined in this section relate to the acquisition and production of evidence, the interpretation of evidence and arguments, the presentation of evidence and arguments and their application to sociological debates. (Evidence is taken to include both primary and secondary sources as well as both quantitative and qualitative data.)

Collection and recording of evidence

Candidates are also required to demonstrate their ability to:

- analyse and evaluate the design of sociological investigations
- analyse and evaluate the method(s) used in these investigations to collect and record evidence

Interpretation and evaluation of evidence

Candidates must demonstrate their ability to:

- distinguish between facts, opinions and value judgements
- select and apply a range of relevant concepts and theories
- interpret qualitative and quantitative data
- identify and evaluate significant social trends shown in evidence
- evaluate theories, arguments and evidence

Presentation of evidence and argument

Candidates must demonstrate their ability to:

- organise evidence and communicate arguments in a coherent manner
- demonstrate an awareness and understanding of theoretical sociological debates
- use evidence to support and sustain arguments and conclusions

New to Unit 2 is the incorporation of research methods in the context of education. Alongside the development of your knowledge and understanding of the sociology of education, it will be essential to understand how research evidence has been gained and what methods have been used to produce the evidence. You will need to demonstrate your ability to apply, interpret and analyse the research methods and data available within the topic and, perhaps most importantly, show the ability to evaluate methods, sources and evidence.

The skill of evaluation is an important one, and should be applied to all the material you come across during your study of a topic. In practice, this means that you should develop the habit of asking questions, such as:

'How did they find that out?'

'Is there any other evidence of this?'

'What are the strengths and limitations of any method?'

'Which sociologists disagree with this view?'

In more practical terms, it means that whenever you are introduced to a sociological perspective or study, you should consider *two or three* criticisms that have been made of it. You should also remember, of course, which group or person has made these criticisms, as this is important knowledge and can be used to evaluate the method.

As well as the above skills, you must:

- be well organised so that your arguments are coherent
- show an awareness of the theoretical debates in sociology
- use evidence to support and sustain your arguments and conclusions

Study skills and revision strategies

- Good revision equals good results and, therefore, needs time spent on it.
- As well as reading and making notes, you should try to read a quality newspaper such as the *Guardian*, the *Independent* or the *Observer* at least once a week. The *Guardian* has sections dedicated to society, media and education that are of particular sociological interest. They will provide you with contemporary examples that you can refer to in your essays.
- Surf the net! There are now some excellent websites dedicated to AS and A-level Sociology.
- If you do not already subscribe to *Sociology Review*, your school or college library probably does. Read back copies. This magazine is invaluable for keeping you up to date with sociological research and for giving good advice on exams.
- For each of your AS units, make sure that you know what the examination board specifies as necessary knowledge. Make notes on each of these areas and keep them in a revision folder separate from your class notes.
- Be organised! Make yourself an examination and revision timetable divided into topics, well before the exams start.
- When you finally reach the week(s) of the exams, get a good night's sleep each night. Do *not* stay up until the early hours trying to get in some last-minute revision.
- In the exam, allocate your time carefully. Make sure that you have enough time to write answers to all of the questions asked of you and give yourself sufficient time for essay-type answers.

The unit examination

Education is a Unit 2 topic. This unit also contains the topic of Health, and both Education and Health will be taught alongside Sociological Methods. The unit exam paper is allocated 2 hours and is divided into two sections.

Section A is Education and Section B is Health, but candidates choose to answer questions on only *one* of these topics. For each section the examination paper has three questions and you must answer all of them.

- **Question 1** is on your chosen topic, in this case Education. This question is divided into four parts and there are 40 marks in total.
- **Question 2** refers to sociological research methods in the context of education. This is a one-part question and is awarded 20 marks.
- **Question 3** is on freestanding research methods. It is in four parts and is awarded 30 marks in total.

So the raw marks for the paper as a whole total 90. The unit as a whole is worth 60% of the AS qualification and 30% of the total A-level qualification.

Questions 1 and 2 on the examination paper will feature source material, or 'items' — one for each question. These are designed to help you by providing information on which you may draw in your answer. It is therefore essential that you read the items carefully, and continue to refer to them when asked.

Sometimes a question will make a specific reference to an item, such as 'With reference to Item A', or 'Using material from Item B and elsewhere'. In these cases you should make quite sure that you clearly follow the instruction. An easy way of doing this is to say, for example:
'The view referred to in Item A is that...'
'Item A shows evidence of...'
'Item B gives examples of...'
'The view in Item B reflects the Marxist view of..., which has been criticised, particularly by functionalists, who argue that...'.

Questions 1 and 3 are broken down into a number of parts, usually (a) to (d), each with its own mark allocation. In question 1 the four-part questions will add up to 40, whereas in question 3 they will add up to 30 marks. Question 1(c) is in the form of a mini-essay and will be assessed as 8 marks for AO1 and 4 for AO2. The higher the mark allocation, the more you would normally need to write to gain full marks and the more time you need to allocate to it.

Content Guidance

This section outlines the major issues and themes of **Education and Sociological Methods**. These are offered as guidance only; there are other concepts and studies that may be relevant. With regard to studies, your textbooks will contain sufficient examples for your needs. Back copies of *Sociology Review* will also provide a number of useful articles.

The content of **Education** falls into five main areas:
- the role and purpose of education, including vocational education and training, in contemporary society
- differential educational achievement of social groups by social class, gender and ethnicity in contemporary society
- relationships and processes within schools, with particular reference to teacher/pupil relationships, pupil subcultures, the hidden curriculum, and the organisation of teaching and learning
- the significance of educational policies, including selection, comprehensivisation and marketisation, for an understanding of the structure, role, impact and experience of education
- the application of sociological research methods to the study of education

The topic of **Education** is designed to give you a good understanding of the historical development of education and its importance within society today. You will need to know different explanations of the role of the education system. This will include perspectives such as functionalist, Marxist, feminist and New Right. You will also be expected to discuss various explanations of the differing educational achievement by social class, gender and ethnic groups and be familiar with the empirical evidence for them. Another important area is what happens within schools, including teacher/pupil relationships, pupil subcultures, the hidden curriculum and the organisation of teaching and learning. The other major section is the significance of state policies for an understanding of the role, impact and experience of education. The core themes are integrated within the topic. You will, however, need to be familiar with sociological research methods and evidence, types of data, their strengths and weaknesses, and why researchers choose the methods that they use.

You can expect to be tested on:
- quantitative and qualitative methods of research; their strengths and limitations; research design
- sources of data, and their strengths and limitations
- the distinction between primary and secondary, and quantitative and qualitative data
- the relationship between perspectives and sociological methods; the nature of 'social facts'
- theoretical, practical and ethical considerations influencing choice of topic and method(s)

Explanations of the role and purpose of education, including vocational education, in contemporary society

Functionalist

Key ideas

- Education is seen as the main agency of secondary socialisation, taking over as the focal socialising agency after the family. Children are socialised by their families and later by their schools, into the value consensus; that is, into a system of shared values that underpin the society.
- Education provides a bridge between the home and the wider society. In school, children are judged by the universalistic standards of society rather than the particularistic values of the home. At school, each student is treated as an individual on their own merits; whereas at home children are related to as sons/daughters/brothers/sisters etc.
- Education is meritocratic. This means that it acts as a neutral filter ensuring that all pupils receive education suited to their natural aptitudes. Those who achieve do so through their own talents, attitudes and application to work.
- Education performs the vital task of role allocation. The most able and talented must be filtered into the most functionally important positions in society.
- Education reinforces social solidarity in society.

Evaluation

+ Identifies education as an integral part of the social structure.
+ Acknowledges the vital role of education as an agency of secondary socialisation.
+ Identifies the needs of modern industrial societies to have an appropriately skilled workforce produced by the education system.
– Marxists argue that:
  - meritocracy is a myth, transmitted by the ruling class to make the system appear to be fair and just
  - education transmits the values and ideology of the dominant class
  - education reproduces the next generation of workers for capitalism

Key concepts

meritocracy; role allocation; secondary socialisation; social solidarity; transmission of shared norms and values

Key thinkers
Durkheim, Parsons, Davis and Moore

Marxist

Key ideas

- Meritocracy is a myth.
- Education is a major agency of social control in modern capitalist society.
- The education system is an ideological state apparatus that brainwashes children into docility and obedience.
- The hidden curriculum ensures that the values and ideology of the dominant class are internalised as natural and normal by pupils.
- Education reproduces the next generation of workers for capitalism.
- The relationship between teachers and pupils mirrors the exploitative relationship between bosses and workers.
- The economic infrastructure exerts considerable influence over the schooling system. There is a close correspondence between the needs of capitalism and the schooling system.
- The class system is reproduced through the schooling system. Educational inequality is systematic and the real task of the schooling system is to filter working-class pupils into working-class jobs. Middle-class pupils are filtered into middle-class jobs and the professions.

Evaluation

+ Identifies the education system as shaped by structural factors. Recognises the influence of the economy in how education is shaped and delivered.
+ Much sociological research supports the Marxist claim that working-class pupils are not encouraged to succeed in school.
+ Recognises the importance of ideology in education.
+ Identifies the myth of meritocracy.
- The focus is too class-based. Gender and ethnicity tend to be ignored.
- Overemphasises docility and obedience from pupils. Bowles and Gintis, as well as Althusser, have tended to underestimate pupil resistance to teachers and school.
- Overstates the close connection between the needs of capitalism and the type of school system.

Key concepts

cultural capital; cultural reproduction; hidden curriculum; ideological state apparatus; myth of meritocracy; reproduction of workers for capitalism; social control

Key thinkers

Bowles and Gintis, Bourdieu, Boudon, Althusser, Willis, Braverman, Farkas

Feminist

Key ideas

- Education reproduces patriarchal power in society.
- The curriculum is still biased in favour of white middle-class male knowledge.
- Textbooks and reading schemes still have a male bias.
- Teachers of both sexes give boys more classroom attention than they give girls.
- The hidden curriculum reinforces gender socialisation.
- Subject choice in secondary school is still gendered.
- Sexual harassment of girls and women teachers by male pupils is a major feature of mixed schools.
- Despite the introduction of the National Curriculum, gender stereotyping in education is still widespread.

Evaluation

- + Identifies the education system as a major agency of gender socialisation.
- + Identifies gender as a key factor in educational inequality.
- + Feminist studies indicated that boys demanded and received more teacher-time than girls.
- + Identifies the fact that power in society is patriarchal.
- − Traditional feminist explanations focused on the reasons for the perceived under-achievement of girls, but this is seen as less relevant today as girls have been outperforming boys over the past 20 years.
- − Boys are now the underachievers. Recent feminist research has focused on the coping strategies of girls in school, their identity formation and career options.
- − Girls' attitudes towards the importance of education have changed (see Sharpe's study).

Key concepts

gender socialisation; male domination of the classroom; patriarchal curriculum; sexual harassment; subject choice

Key thinkers

Sharpe, Spender, Kelly, Stanworth, Deem, Jones and Mahony, Delamont, Lees, Warrington and Younger

The New Right

Key ideas

- Market forces should be introduced into schooling. Successful schools are rewarded with higher budgets to increase their roll while failing schools are closed down. Schools are encouraged to compete in the marketplace for clients (that is, pupils).

- There is an increased focus on vocational education and preparing pupils for the world of work. The introduction of General National Vocational Qualifications (GNVQs), compulsory work experience for year 10 pupils and the National Record of Achievement (NRA) for all year 11 pupils were implemented in order to achieve this.
- National testing at the various key stages was introduced.
- League tables to show comparative results for schools are published.
- Schools have greater control over their budgets and less involvement with the local education authority (LEA).
- Parents have the right to choose the school to which they would like to send their child.
- A greater focus is put on school inspection to ensure rising standards in all state schools.

Evaluation

Many commentators have concentrated on the negative aspects of the New Right reforms. However, it is important to produce a balance to your evaluation.

+ The reforms give parents more information about the performance of their children's schools.
+ Ofsted identifies schools with particular problems and suggests and monitors improvements.
+ Schools are more aware of the needs of employers.
− Stephen Ball et al. argue that New Right reforms to education have served to make education less egalitarian and far more divisive, because they give an advantage to middle-class parents. This is because middle-class parents have cultural capital and are therefore more likely to make a favourable impression on the head teacher at interview. Also, these parents understand the schooling system and they can afford to move into middle-class catchment areas where there are successful schools high in the league tables.
− Marxists such as Finn argue that the focus on new vocationalism and youth training is simply reproducing young workers for capitalism who have been socialised into the right attitudes and are ready for exploitation.
− British children are subjected to more tests than their European counterparts.

Key concepts

competition; league tables; marketisation of education; parental choice; pupil testing; standards, training, vocationalism

Key thinkers
Chubb and Moe, Finn

Interactionist

Key ideas

- Interactionists examine education from a micro-perspective. The focus is on the day-to-day running of schools and the interaction between teachers and pupils and between pupils and pupils within the classroom.
- The classroom is constructed and constantly renegotiated through interaction between teachers and pupils. Pupils are not passive recipients of teachers' knowledge, but actively participate in learning and resistance.
- Teachers play a crucial role in the success of their students, because they can affect the self-concepts and self-esteem of students.
- The labelling and typing of students by teachers can lead to the creation of self-fulfilling prophecies.
- Streaming and setting have significant effects on the success of pupils in school. There is a close relationship between banding and the social-class background of pupils.
- Some pupils resist the school system. This resistance takes different forms, varying from active rebellion and aggression to subtle adaptations of behaviour.
- Peer groups are seen as having considerable influence on some pupils. This influence can have positive or negative effects on behaviour and achievement.

Evaluation

- \+ Interactionists have challenged the rather deterministic approaches of Marxism and functionalism to education.
- \+ They have provided valuable insights into the day-to-day running of schools and the reality of the classroom.
- \+ They have demonstrated the importance of teachers in the success or failure of their pupils.
- – Interactionists have been accused of determinism in their approach to education. They presume that once a label has been applied to somebody, a self-fulfilling prophecy will follow.
- – The narrow focus on interaction within the school ignores the importance of wider structural constraints in educational success.
- – Many ethnographic studies tend to be descriptive rather than explanatory.

Key concepts

interaction; labelling; negotiation; pupil adaptations; pupil subcultures; self-concept; self-fulfilling prophecy; typing

Key thinkers

Becker, Hargreaves, Hester and Mellor, Keddie, Rosenthal and Jacobson, Woods, Ball, Padfield, Hattersley and French

Vocationalism

Vocationalism is the link between education and the labour market. It stems from the belief that education should be the training ground for employment and it is often associated with ideas of the New Right. It is argued that education and training should help to promote economic growth by teaching the skills needed by the workforce. In the 1980s, a 'new vocationalism' developed under the Conservative governments led by Margaret Thatcher, during which a number of new measures were introduced.

- The Technical and Vocational Education Initiative (TVEI) was introduced in 1983 and extended nationally for all 14- to 18-year-old students. It broadened the curriculum and emphasised the importance of work experience for all.
- The Certificate of Pre-Vocational Education (CPVE) was introduced in 1985. Less academically able students were taught practical skills in order to prepare them for employment.
- National Vocational Qualifications and General National Vocational Qualifications (NVQs and GNVQs), introduced in 1993, remain on the curriculum and include leisure and tourism, business, information technology, health and social care.
- Training and Enterprise Councils (TECs) began in 1990 and are led by local business people who receive money for skills training to meet local needs. However, there is controversy over their efficacy.
- Youth Training Schemes (YTSs) were designed for school leavers as a form of employment training rather than work experience. Young people are given opportunities to gain qualifications.

Evaluation

+ Left Modernisers argue that education standards need to be as high as possible in order to produce a 'magnet economy', where the skills and productivity of the workforce will encourage overseas investment.

+ Instituting appropriate skills training and retraining programmes will give individuals better chances of finding employment.

+ It could be a means of increased opportunities as skill inequalities will be reduced.

However, many criticisms have been levelled at the schemes:

- They are used to restrict the number of workers joining trade unions, in this way reducing the potential bargaining power of the unions.
- The trainees are a source of cheap labour.
- The trainees are not counted as unemployed even though they have no guarantee of paid employment after the scheme is over.
- New workers are kept in 'suspended animation' until jobs become available.
- Trainees are substitutes for full-time workers who would have to be paid more.
- Trainees are potentially de-skilled by being taught 'behavioural etiquette' rather than transferable skills — in this way they have been prepared for disempowerment.

– Strathdee (2003) argued that in relation to vocational education and training (VET), Labour policies have strengthened previous Conservative policies in using the New Deal punitively to pressurise young people to participate or lose benefit entitlements. Even though there have been well-intentioned attempts to raise the status of VET, it remains a route into lower-paid, less skilled work primarily for working-class youth.

Key concepts

youth training schemes; TVEI; NVQs; GNVQs

Key thinkers

Finn, Bates et al., Yeomans

Sociological explanations of the differential educational achievements of social groups by social class, gender and ethnicity

This is a large area within the topic of Education and is likely to produce a variety of questions on the examination paper. It is extremely important to be aware of the factors that affect differential achievement.

Other significant factors affecting both achievement and underachievement lie within schools themselves. These are dealt with later in the guide.

Social class

Outside-school explanations

Poverty and material deprivation leading to poor educational achievement

Poverty and low income are likely to result in fewer books and educational toys in the home, as well as a lower likelihood of computer access. There may be overcrowding and children will have no adequate study area at home. Poverty might result in damp homes that can lead to bronchial infections, more illness and increased time off school. Structural material explanations for inequalities in health see material deprivation as a key factor. Jesson and Gray's 1991 Nottinghamshire study identified a clear correlation between poverty and material deprivation. Half of the pupils receiving free school meals attained GCSE scores below 15 points as opposed to one sixth of pupils who paid for meals. Underclass theory is also important here. Phillips (2001) has shown that the 'socially excluded' pupils are not simply poor, but the consequence of family attitudes and values that are anti-education and a state system that both encourages dependency and undermines individual responsibility.

Home factors and parental interest

Douglas saw parental interest as the single most important factor affecting pupil progress. He argued that in general, middle-class parents were more interested in the progress of their children than were working-class parents. Parental interest was measured by visits to the school and how teachers viewed parents. However, this approach has been criticised for failing to take into account different work practices of parents and less knowledge of the education system. Reay has argued that unlike many working-class parents, many middle-class parents, especially mothers, invest 'emotional labour' in their children's education.

Culture clash

Cultural deficit theorists have maintained that working-class families place great emphasis on immediate gratification and the need to find employment at the minimum school leaving age, whereas middle-class families place most emphasis on educational success and staying on post-16. Some working-class pupils may face a culture clash between the values of home and school.

Language difference

Bernstein identified two different speech codes: the **elaborated** and **restricted** codes. He argued that working-class pupils are generally socialised into a restricted language code where meanings are context-bound and sentences short with limited vocabulary. Middle-class children, however, have access to both codes. As the language of the school and teachers is of an elaborated nature, this works to the benefit of middle-class pupils.

Cultural capital

According to Bourdieu, inequalities in power and wealth in society account for the inequalities in educational achievement. Bourdieu argues that children from middle- and upper-class backgrounds have been socialised into the dominant culture and possess cultural capital. Their pre-school socialisation has been much closer to the dominant culture and the values of the school than that of working-class children. The dominant class has the power to impose its culture and values as legitimate and the curriculum reflects these values and interests. Working-class children are filtered out of the education system at earliest school leaving age through two processes: failure in examinations, and self-elimination. They give up on school because it is so alien to them. Recent research by Reay et al. (2008 ongoing) has shown the continuing significance of cultural capital to achievement. Middle-class students in underachieving schools still do very well, and in many cases do better than similar students in predominantly middle-class schools, because the schools treat them as potential achievers, often placing them on Gifted and Talented registers.

Positional theory

Marxist sociologist Raymond Boudon argues that educational inequality is inevitable because of social stratification. Students start school from very different positions, depending on their class. Boudon refers to a cost–benefit analysis of education, whereby studying for higher education may have very different consequences for a middle-class student than for a working-class student. The parents of middle-class students are much more likely to be able to support them financially and to encourage them to follow a profession. However, working-class parents are far less likely to have the material resources to support their son or daughter through university. University fees currently exceed £1,200 per annum. A working-class student who goes to university, particularly Oxford or Cambridge, will also encounter a significantly different culture from that of home. Working-class students might therefore resist or reject higher education.

Inside-school explanations

Labelling and self-fulfilling prophecy

Teachers are middle class by virtue of their profession and will generally support middle-class values and attitudes. These values may well be at odds with those of some working-class children. Becker's work demonstrated that teachers tended to see middle-class pupils as those closer to the ideal. Keddie's work showed that social class and streaming are closely linked. Pupils from lower working-class backgrounds were predominantly found in lower streams at school. Teachers withheld knowledge that was essential for success from these groups, believing that these students could not handle such complex knowledge. Teachers might stereotype working-class pupils as unlikely to stay on and therefore have lower expectations of these pupils. This may well lead to a self-fulfilling prophecy whereby those children will become less interested in what schooling has to offer and give up on education. It is interesting to see that the introduction of league tables has inadvertently discouraged the progress of lower-ability students. Robinson (1998) demonstrated that although overall rates of achievement had risen, the lower-ability pupils had suffered because teachers concentrate on moving potentially grade-D GCSE students to grade-Cs and neglect those who are lower down the achievement ladder.

Key concepts

economic capital; cultural capital; elaborated and restricted language codes; immediate and deferred gratification; fatalism; cultural reproduction; meritocracy

Key thinkers

Halsey, Bernstein, Douglas, Bourdieu, Ball, Keddie, Sugarman, Hyman, Willis, Becker, Rist, Boudon, Reay

Gender

Gender issues before 1980

- Sociological explanations of gender and educational achievement before the 1980s focused on the underachievement of girls.
- The educational ideology reflected that of the wider, patriarchal society which emphasised the domestic role of women. As a result, many girls (apart from a few who went on to be university-educated) were encouraged to take up those subjects that would fit them for their assumed future roles as wives and mothers.
- Goldstein argued that the selection for the tripartite system by 11-plus examination was not an equitable system, as many grammar school places which should have been taken by girls were given to boys in order to even up the numbers of boy and girl pupils. Girls' results were weighted downwards to give boys an equal chance of a grammar school place.
- The career aspirations of girls were seen as less significant than those of boys.
- Socialisation practices at home were seen as detrimental to the career prospects of girls. Gender socialisation encouraged passivity and gentleness in girls and aggression and an instrumental attitude in boys.
- Research into school socialisation focused on reading schemes (Lobban) and discovered a considerable amount of gender-stereotyped material.

Gender issues after 1980

- Over the past two decades, there has been a significant increase in the achievement of girls, especially at GCSE. In 2000, girls were also ahead of boys at A-level and the gap between the genders had increased. New explanations have been put forward as to why this reversal of fortunes has taken place and the focus has changed to explaining the underachievement of boys.
- Although girls have overtaken boys in public examinations, gender differences in subject choices remain. This is most apparent in post-16 science and technology, which are chosen by more boys than girls.
- In higher education there are also changes. In 1996/97 men were more likely than women to gain first degrees in sciences (other than social and biological sciences), engineering and architecture, building and planning. However, in all but a minority of other subjects, women predominated. Women have now overtaken men in medicine, dentistry, business and finance degrees.
- Colley (1998) found that despite the National Curriculum there are still significant gender differences remaining in option choices. She argues that this is affected by the students' perceptions of subjects.

Inside-school factors affecting the achievement of boys and girls

- State initiatives in the early 1980s were directed at the enhancement of girls' achievement. Examples include WISE (women into science and engineering), GIST (girls into science and technology) and some of the early Technical and Vocational Educational Initiative (TVEI) programmes.

- The increase in service-sector jobs has enhanced the employment opportunities for women.
- The women's movement and feminism may have influenced the aspirations of girls and the increasing independence of women may have filtered down into schools.
- The introduction of coursework was said to help girls as they had different study skills to boys.
- The introduction of the National Curriculum ensured that girls could no longer drop out of traditionally masculine subjects like science and mathematics.
- Laddish behaviour in the classroom and the more general anti-learning, anti-school attitudes of teenage boys has been seen as a means of off-setting generally poor levels of esteem they get from staff and girls (Francis 2000).

Outside-school factors affecting males and females

- Changes in attitudes: the introduction of a laddish culture (including magazines for young men and the rise of football chat-shows on television) in the 1990s, which viewed schoolwork as 'uncool'.
- Changes in the labour market: an increase in unemployment for young men, together with the decline of traditional manufacturing industries. The situation is especially acute for white working-class boys. In 2007 these boys accounted for almost half of students leaving school with low qualifications or with no exam passes at all.
- Changes in the family, such as increased divorce and lone-parenting, have led to a lack of effective role models for many boys and encouraged the idea of economic independence for young women.
- Gender issues are affected by class and ethnicity too, as some social groups — especially Chinese, African and middle-class Asian girls — achieve much higher standards than others.

Key concepts

femininity/masculinity; feminism; gender socialisation; laddism; malestream; nature vs nurture; patriarchy; sexism

Key thinkers

Sharpe, Stanworth, Deem, Spender, Kelly, Delamont, Rutherford, Mac an Ghaill

Ethnicity

While it is true that some ethnic minorities underachieve in the British education system, it is a mistaken generalisation to argue that this is true of all ethnic minorities. The highest achievers in terms of educational qualifications are students from

Indian and Chinese backgrounds and Asian students from East African backgrounds. Although the performance of black Caribbean and Pakistani and Bangladeshi students has improved considerably over the past decade, boys from these ethnic groups still underachieve. (It is important to remember that it is white working-class boys who are the lowest achievers at present.)

There are three broad explanations for the differing attainment of ethnic minorities in the education system: **genetic explanations (non-sociological)**, **inside-school explanations** and **outside-school explanations**.

Genetic explanations

Genetic explanations start with the premise that intelligence is largely inherited and therefore fixed. It is very important to understand that these views are highly criticised by sociologists. On the basis of IQ tests, psychologists such as Jenson and Eysenck have argued that black people have less inherited intelligence than white people. They have been criticised for legitimising racial inequality. Understandably their work has been strongly challenged by sociologists who argue that it is impossible to isolate inheritance from environmental factors such as poverty and racism. For some students these are far more important in relation to their educational success. It is impossible to equalise environmental factors because black people have experienced centuries of racist oppression. Despite having been rejected by sociologists, these genetic explanations still remain.

Inside-school explanations

Curriculum bias and ethnocentrism

Subjects such as English literature, history and religious education have been accused of being ethnocentric. The foci of these subjects have tended to be the achievements of white European (Christian) peoples. The National Curriculum does not include the history of black people, and foreign languages taught in school are primarily European. Where other languages are taught these tend to be extracurricular.

Teacher expectations

Much research has indicated that teachers have lower expectations of black boys than they have of other pupils. These pupils tend to be stereotyped as troublemakers and seen as disruptive. Some sociologists would argue that this labelling is likely to result in a self-fulfilling prophecy.

Institutional racism

In 1999, Ofsted published a damning report on British education, claiming that there was institutional racism within the system. (An institution is described as institutionally racist if its policies and personnel discriminate against a particular minority group.) This claim echoed earlier criticisms expressed in the 1985 Swann Report, which claimed that unintentional racism was a feature of many schools. In the 1970s Bernard Coard argued that the British education system made black Caribbean pupils 'educationally subnormal'. He argued that the system diminished the self-esteem of black Caribbean children.

As Blair et al. show (2003), there is a marked lack of black role models in British schools. Sociologists have also pointed to the lack of ethnic minority head teachers. Recent sociological evidence confirms that many ethnic minority students receive more negative criticism and stereotyping from staff than do white students whether this is intentional or not.

Pupil exclusions

Statistics indicate that all pupil exclusions have risen markedly since the 1980s. This may be due to a range of factors including the focus on school league tables and the reduction in specialist support for pupils with behavioural and learning difficulties. However, Afro-Caribbean pupils are significantly over-represented in exclusion figures. Explanations focus on teacher attitudes, for example seeing black pupils as more disruptive, and on black pupils expressing their frustration in the classroom at the effects of poverty and racism.

Outside-school explanations

Racism

It is impossible to isolate racism in the school from the experience of living in a racist society. All pupils from black, Asian and refugee backgrounds face the threat of racial abuse and attack in Britain. Victimisation studies indicate that Asians are 50 times more likely to be the victims of a racist attack than white people, while black people are 36 times more likely to be victims.

Home factors and parental interest

Cultural deprivation models have placed the blame for educational underachievement on the home. Afro-Caribbean home life has been stereotyped as more stressful, with higher proportions of lone parents and lower family incomes. Pryce claimed that family life among West Indians in Bristol was 'turbulent'. In contrast, Asian families are seen to be a positive resource for their children, with greater emphasis on educational success.

Language factors

In the past, language factors were seen to be significant constraints for both Afro-Caribbean and Asian pupils. It was claimed that pupils coming from homes where English was not the first language were disadvantaged. However, recent research by Driver and Ballard rejects this explanation and the Swann Report did not emphasise this view.

Social class

It is well documented that differences in social class affect the educational attainment of pupils. There are marked socioeconomic differences between ethnic minorities in Britain. As far back as 1985, the Swann Report identified socio-economic factors as being important in the underachievement of children from Afro-Caribbean backgrounds. In 2007 boys from these backgrounds still fared worse educationally than Afro-Caribbean girls and white students. It is probable that the growing number of violent youth gangs on lower socioeconomic estates may have a deleterious influence on the educational success of these boys.

Criticisms/racism reconsidered

Fuller's research showed that black girls did not accept negative teacher expectations and that they fought the labels to achieve success. Stone's research questioned the view that black pupils have low self-esteem. Many pupils in the study were hostile to teachers yet maintained a positive self-image.

Prejudice among teachers might be expressed in the staff room but might not necessarily extend into the classroom.

Key concepts

labelling and the self-fulfilling prophecy; ethnocentrism; institutional racism; resistance; curriculum bias

Key thinkers

Wright, Coard, Fuller, Mirza, Pilkington, Brittan, Driver and Ballard, Pryce, Mac an Ghaill

Relationships and processes in schools (teacher/pupil relationships; pupil subcultures; the hidden curriculum and the organisation of teaching and learning)

Teacher/pupil relationships

Key ideas

- Labelling.
- Self-fulfilling prophecy.
- Teacher expectations — linked to:
  - social class
  - gender
  - ethnicity

(These are all discussed earlier in the guide.)

Pupil subcultures

Key ideas

Subcultures are created through processes within the school such as streaming and labelling.

- Some teachers label lower-stream students as 'failures'. The students attempt to protect their self-identity and self-worth by forming subcultures. Understanding the development of subcultures tends to come from the interactionist approach.
- Early theorists like Cohen and Miller explained the creation of subcultures as resulting from status frustration and the focal concerns of working-class boys. It was assumed that as they were unlikely to be successful within the education system, they would find status outside the classroom.
- Later researchers such as Woods have argued that pupils' adaptations to the experience of school life depend on acceptance or rejection of the importance of academic success. Woods has identified eight adaptations: ingratiation, compliance, opportunism, ritualism, retreatism, colonisation, intransigence and rebellion. He has related these adaptations to social class by arguing that middle-class students tend to have the more conformist adaptations, whereas working-class pupils show the least conformist adaptations.

Resistance and failure

Willis, from a Marxist perspective, identified two discernible subcultures: the 'lads' and the 'ear'oles'. The lads accorded no value to the education system and qualifications but felt themselves to be superior to the ear'oles who were prepared to be compliant in school in order to gain skilled employment later. Although the lads claimed to resist and 'have a laff at' the system, ironically it was preparing them for low-skilled manual work.

Resistance and success

Fuller's study of a group of Afro-Caribbean girls in a London comprehensive demonstrated another form of resistance. The girls, labelled as failures by their teacher, rejected the negative label and worked hard to ensure their success. Fuller's work is important in showing that subcultural resistance does not necessarily mean academic failure.

Evaluation

- + Draws attention to the importance of peer groups and subcultures.
- + Gives another aspect of the influence of in-school factors on underachievement.
- − Takes a relatively deterministic approach to the development of subcultures. It is possible that at times even the more conformist pupils will become deviant and disruptive if teachers are seen to be lacking classroom discipline.

– Not all teachers adopt a middle-class view of the world and might be more sympathetic to the anti-authoritarianism of some pupils.

Key concepts

delinquent subcultures; labelling; resistance; self-fulfilling prophecy; streaming

Key thinkers

Hargreaves, Woods, Willis, Fuller, Mac an Ghaill

The organisation of teaching and learning

Key ideas

- Social policies relating to education emphasise teaching and learning rather than just teaching.
- Teaching and learning styles: the emphasis in education changed from the process of teachers **teaching** students to one where students' learning processes became prominent. This emphasised the different ways in which individuals learn, including multiple intelligences, personalised learning and the use and impact of new technologies in the classroom.
- Switching-on: successful pupils learn how to please the teacher.
- Switching-off: pupils fail to conform to teachers' expectations and do not value what is being taught.

Key thinkers

Cano-Garcia and Hughes, Barrett

Educational policies (including selection, comprehensivisation and marketisation)

1870 Education Act

The 1870 Forster Act introduced elementary education for all 5- to 10-year-olds. By 1880 it was compulsory for all children to be educated to the age of 10. A limited curriculum was offered focusing on the importance of the 'four Rs': reading, writing, arithmetic and religion.

Over the twentieth century the school leaving age was gradually raised to 16 years. However, social class and education were clearly linked. Until the Second World War, there were three broad types of school, according to social class:

- elementary schools for the working class
- grammar schools for the middle classes (these were fee-paying institutions)
- public schools for the upper classes

1944 Education Act

The 1944 Butler Act was a fundamental part of the creation of the welfare state and introduced free state education for all pupils in England and Wales from the age of 5 up to 15 years. The aim of the Act was to provide equality of educational opportunity for all children, regardless of their socioeconomic background. The Act introduced the tripartite system whereby all state pupils took an examination at 11. On the basis of this test, pupils were allocated to one of three types of secondary school: grammar, secondary modern or technical.

Grammar schools

These schools were intended for the academically able and were modelled on the public schools. Only 20% of the school population attended grammar school and their intake was predominantly middle class. Pupils had to pass the 11-plus examination to attend.

Secondary modern schools

Approximately 75% of children attended this type of school, which offered a basic education and little opportunity to take external exams. Approximately 80% of secondary modern pupils left without any qualifications.

Technical schools

These schools emphasised vocational subjects and technical skills. There were very few technical schools built and they were attended by only 5% of the school population.

Criticisms of the tripartite system

Parity of esteem

The tripartite system was founded on the idea of separate but equal types of school for the different aptitudes and abilities of students. However, in reality grammar schools were afforded much higher status than secondary modern and technical schools. Few technical schools were built and the system was really bipartite rather than tripartite.

Low self-esteem

The system resulted in educational success or failure at age 11. Failing the 11-plus created low self-esteem in children and turned them off schooling at an early age. Sociologists argue that once labelled a failure at 11 this created a self-fulfilling prophecy. The 11-plus system was responsible for a huge wastage of educational talent, since the majority of secondary modern students left school with no qualifications. Sociologists have been highly critical of the validity of IQ testing. They believe that these tests are not valid indicators of intelligence but are culturally biased and ethnocentric.

Social class

Although the system was designed to remove class barriers to education and ensure that every pupil went to the school best suited to his or her aptitudes, in reality there was a very strong correlation between social class and secondary school. Grammar schools were for the most part middle-class institutions, leaving working-class children to a second-rate education in a secondary modern.

Comprehensivisation

By the 1960s, concerns were being raised that the tripartite system had not achieved its aim to democratise education and that the class system was still very much intact. The goal of the tripartite system to produce a meritocracy had failed. In response, the Labour government proposed the introduction of comprehensive schools, which were designed to introduce more social mixing and eradicate testing at 11. In 1965, the Labour government required all local education authorities (LEAs) to submit plans to show how they would become comprehensive. This was a very slow business and one that was opposed by the Conservatives. However, by 1974, 80% of secondary pupils attended a comprehensive school.

Criticisms of comprehensivisation

- Standards have been lowered and higher-ability children have been held back.
- Comprehensivisation has not succeeded in more social mixing, as class differences persist in terms of educational attainment and staying on rates post-16.
- Comprehensives have also failed to produce a meritocracy.

There are significant differences in the pass rates of comprehensives depending on their catchment area. Schools in middle-class areas tend to have much higher pass rates than those in predominantly working-class areas. The 1990s saw further attacks on state schooling by Ofsted. Schools were assessed according to strict guidelines and some were seen as not meeting the various criteria for success. The language and systems of the business world entered education and came to be known as the 'marketisation of education'. Schools are now in competition with each other for pupils and ultimately for their own survival.

Responses to the criticisms

- Educational pass rates have risen significantly since the 1960s. Today many more children leave school with qualifications than did in the tripartite system.
- Evidence suggests that children of the highest academic ability do as well in comprehensives as in other types of state school.
- The state system has always had to compete with private schools and grammar schools. In many areas, private and grammar schools have 'creamed off' the brightest children, while the assisted-places scheme introduced by the Conservatives in 1980 allowed less affluent 'gifted' children to attend a private school without having to pay the fees. Even here the assisted places went overwhelmingly to middle-class children.

1988 Education Reform Act

The 1988 Education Reform Act has had the most significant impact on schooling since 1944. It introduced a set of far-reaching reforms on education.

National Curriculum

For the first time in Britain the government decided which subjects should be studied in all state schools. English, Maths and Science became core subjects for all 11- to 16-year-olds and it also became compulsory for all secondary school students to study a foreign language.

Parental choice

The Act encouraged parents to choose a secondary school for their child. Critics argue that, in reality, this choice only increased the social divisions in schools and allowed middle-class parents to play the system to their advantage.

National testing

With the aim of raising national standards, testing and national attainment targets were introduced for children at ages 7, 11, 14 and 16.

City technology colleges

These were inner-city schools that specialised in technology and were partly funded by the private sector. They were independent of the LEA.

Local management of schools (LMS)

The Act changed the nature of funding for schools. LMS meant that each school had more power over its budget. The responsibility for managing the budget was removed from the LEA and given to the head teacher and the governors.

New Labour and educational policy

Since 1997, New Labour has emphasised the links between education and work. Its policies have been referred to as post-Fordist in that they focus on education in a global market, and view education and training as crucial for economic success. Its policies included the following:

- encouragement of nursery education
- literacy and numeracy hours in primary schools and the setting up of the National Literacy Strategy
- reduction of class sizes to 30 in primary schools
- home–school contracts
- target setting
- Ofsted inspection of schools, including naming and shaming 'failing schools' and direct intervention in such schools by government agencies
- setting up of the Learning and Skills Council (2000) to oversee post-16 education and training in order to improve standards
- setting up education action zones (EAZ) from 1998 together with social exclusion units to tackle problems emerging from areas of high social deprivation (including Sure Start initiatives)
- the New Deal to get the young unemployed and lone parents back to work
- the expansion of specialist schools as 'centres of excellence' in specific subject areas such as arts and media, sports, technology and business
- encouragement of faith schools — usually established by a single faith group
- Curriculum 2000: introduction of AS and A2 rather than a single A-level examination
- Education Maintenance Allowance for 16-year-olds in full-time education
- the setting up of City Academies funded by the state and private enterprise
- social inclusion: vocational education and work experience for disaffected school students, Excellence in Cities, Sure Start, Extended Schools, New Start
- Tomlinson Report (2004) and the introduction of the 14 to 19 Diploma

Evaluation

+ New Labour has retained New Right policies on inspection and parental choice.
- New Right would criticise New Labour for limiting parental choice by abolishing grant-maintained status for schools.
- Liberals would criticise them for taking an overly economic perspective on education.
- Marxists would criticise them for not dealing with inequality of opportunity.
- From a social-democratic perspective, they have failed to abolish selection and have not dealt with setting and streaming.
- Tuition fees for higher education students affect the economically underprivileged more than they affect others.
- The introduction of more selection within education tends to benefit the children of the more culturally advantaged, as poorer children are over-represented in the less academically successful schools.

- Some critics have argued that increasing examination success is a result of exams being 'dumbed down'.
- Whitty (2002) criticised the reforms for allowing the middle class to benefit rather than producing a more egalitarian system.
+ Some policies such as EAZs and the reduction of class sizes reduced inequality in some measure.
+ Trowler (2003) supported many of these policies. He maintained that educational funding had increased significantly; resources for deprived areas were enhanced; the emphasis on lifelong learning and the creation of a learning society were to be applauded as they allowed for those who hadn't achieved at school to realise their potential later.
- However, like all governments before it, New Labour has assumed that the education system is capable of solving social problems and promoting social change. Strathdee (2003) argued that in relation to vocational education and training (VET), Labour policies have strengthened previous Conservative policies in using the New Deal punitively to pressurise young people to participate or lose benefit entitlements. Even though there have been well-intentioned attempts to raise the status of VET, it remains a route into lower-paid, less skilled work primarily for working-class youth.

Sociological research methods

Positivist and interpretivist approaches to research

These approaches influence the methodology that sociologists use in undertaking research.

Positivism

Positivists assume that sociological explanations should be like those of the natural sciences, and that sociologists should use the logic, methods and procedures of natural science.

Key ideas
- Social reality is capable of being measured objectively by using scientific methods.
- As with the natural world, social behaviour is governed by underlying causal laws and can, therefore, be predicted.
- By systematic observation of causal relationships between social phenomena, these laws can be revealed. (An example of the discovery of causal laws can be seen in Durkheim's work on suicide, where he showed that social laws affected an individual's likelihood of suicide.)

+ As far as possible, scientists and sociologists must be personally objective in their research. The resulting data would then be reliable and would not be dependent on the subjectivity of the researcher.

+ Positivists see the need to rely on empirical evidence in testing their assumptions. They argue that assuming what people are thinking is both impossible and inappropriate to the scientific endeavour.

However:

– Positivism fails to understand that individuals create social reality through their interactions.

– It assumes that there is only one view of social reality.

– It does not allow us to see the world from the position of the social actor.

Interpretivism

Unlike positivism, interpretivism rejects the idea that social behaviour can be studied using the same methodology as that of natural science. Interpretivists do not accept a single social reality but see many realities produced through the interactions of individuals. Weber's *verstehen* sociology emphasised that sociologists had to interpret the meanings of social action as understood by the social actors involved. This meant that sociologists needed to put themselves in the position of the person or group being observed.

Key ideas

• The subject matter of sociology is fundamentally different from that of the natural sciences.

• The subjective consciousness of individuals cannot be quantified.

• There is no possibility of gaining understanding of social action through scientific methods.

• Social meanings are the most important aspect of interaction and these need to be understood by sociologists using qualitative methods.

• There are no causal laws governing social behaviour.

• An example of this approach can be seen in Goffman's work on total institutions, where he showed how inmates construct practices to 'make out' in the institution.

Sociological approaches

Phenomenology, social action, symbolic interactionism, feminism, *verstehen* sociology

+ Interpretivism allows us to see that individuals perceive social reality in different ways.

+ Individuals are not passive — they are not seen as simply manipulated by external forces but as active individuals, making choices and acting on social meanings.
− Methods used tend to rely on the subjectivity of the researcher.
− It fails to examine the effects of power differences on social interaction.
− It underestimates the extent and impact of social structure on individuals.

Links to methods

These approaches are linked with specific types of methods in research.

Positivist sociologists see social reality as objective and measurable and tend to favour quantitative methods, such as social surveys using postal or self-administered questionnaires and/or structured interviews. They sometimes, but rarely, undertake laboratory experiments and also make use of official statistics as secondary data. Content analysis of the media is usually quantitative.

Interpretivist sociologists see social reality as constructed by social actors (individuals) through the meanings of social action. They tend to favour qualitative methods such as observation, participant observation, unstructured or semi-structured interviews and field experiments. Secondary data sources are more likely to be personal documents and descriptive historical documents, and also oral histories and self-report studies. Content analysis of the media is qualitative and thematic, and semiology may sometimes be used.

However, many sociologists are increasingly making use of methodological pluralism, that is using more than one method in one research project. This enhances validity, reliability and generalisability.

Methods of sociological research

Methods can be **quantitative**, in which case they produce numerical and statistical data, or **qualitative**, where in-depth, meaning-rich data are gained. They can also be divided into **primary** methods of data collection, where researchers collect the data themselves, and **secondary** methods, where the data have been collected by another (or others) for a purpose other than the present research. Primary and secondary data can be both quantitative and qualitative.

Primary data are collected through **social surveys** using questionnaires and/or interviews; **experiments** including laboratory and field, or by use of the **comparative method** if experiment is not possible; **observation**, including non-participant and participant observation.

Secondary data can take the form of quantitative evidence such as **Official Statistics** or more qualitative evidence such as **personal documents**, for example letters, diaries, photographs, and **historical documents** such as parish records. It is also possible for previous research produced by other sociologists to be used as secondary data. **Content analysis** of mass media material can be both quantitative and qualitative.

In the AS examination, you will be required to answer free-standing questions on research methods as well as questions on research methods used in the context of educational research. This section includes some examples of studies from educational research that you can use in answering questions on methods in an educational context, as well as examples of studies from other substantive areas of sociology.

Primary research methods

Operationalising concepts

Before researchers choose the research method(s) for their study, they need to operationalise the concepts that they are going to research. This means that they must 'translate' the concept into something that can be measured. For example, Blauner, in researching the concept of alienation, divided it into distinct aspects: meaninglessness, powerlessness, normlessness, isolation and self-estrangement. He was then able to research each of these to find levels of alienation.

Sampling techniques

For most sociological studies, the group of people of interest to the sociologist is too large. Consequently, the researcher has to find an appropriate but smaller group of individuals to study. This smaller group is called a sample. There are many different ways in which samples can be selected. It is important to note that the type of sample and the way in which it is chosen may have important consequences for the reliability of the data collected, but first some concepts:

- **research or target population**: the whole group being studied, e.g. all year 10 pupils in one school
- **sampling frame**: the list (if one exists) of names of the entire research population
- **sampling unit**: one individual person or institution taken from the sampling frame

There are several different kinds of sampling procedures, some of which are more representative than others:

- **Representative sampling**: the social characteristics of the sample must resemble those of the research population in, as far as possible, the exact proportion that they occur in that population. So, for example, a sample by gender of a school must have the same proportion of boys and girls as there is in that school.

- **Random sampling**: in a random sample each person or unit has an equal chance of being selected. At its simplest it is a 'picking out of a hat' method. More sophisticated techniques involve random number tables. Simple random sampling will rarely produce representative samples — for instance, randomly choosing a sample of schoolchildren is very unlikely to produce numbers of girls and boys in the same proportion as exists in the school.
- **Stratified random sampling**: this technique is more representative as it divides the research population into specific groups or strata (e.g. all the boys in a school in one group and all the girls in another) and then a sample from each group is randomly selected in the same proportion as they appear in the population.
- **Quota sampling**: this is the usual method used for market research and opinion polls. An interviewer is given a quota of interviews to conduct with individuals fulfilling specific characteristics, e.g. sex, age, social class. The sample is not random, as the choice of interviewees lies with the interviewer. Individuals with the same social characteristics do not have an equal chance of being selected.
- **Multistage samples**: this provides a cheaper and quicker alternative to actual random samples. It involves different stages, at each of which the samples are subdivided. It may be used for opinion polls for example, where constituencies are chosen and then samples are drawn from them.
- **Snowball sampling**: this is used only in cases where there is no sampling frame. The researcher finds his/her interviewees through personal contacts. It is particularly useful when sampling deviant groups, where initial contact with one person can generate further contacts, who can then bring in yet more people.
- **Volunteer sampling**: this is similar to snowball sampling but the researcher may use advertising or leaflets to find contacts. Milgram did this for his obedience to authority experiments.

Each of these sampling techniques has its advantages and disadvantages. So much depends on the nature of the research as to which one the researcher chooses.

Social surveys

Social surveys are the most popular social research method because they can gather a great deal of data from a large section of the population in a relatively short space of time. They most frequently use pre-coded questionnaires, however, some social surveys can also be carried out through interviews.

Ackroyd and Hughes (1981) distinguish between three types of survey:
- factual — the government Census is a factual survey as it collects descriptive data
- attitude — opinion polls come into this category as they collect people's attitudes to events and issues
- explanatory — these are more sociological as they are used to test hypotheses and produce new theories

Questionnaires

A questionnaire is a pre-set, pre-coded list of standardised questions given to a respondent. If an interviewer reads out the questionnaire, it becomes a structured interview (see below). **Postal** questionnaires are mailed to respondents, usually with a stamped addressed envelope or some small incentive to return the form.

Questionnaires produce a large amount of quantitative data and can be given to a widespread target population. For example, the Census is given to every household in the country.

Questions can be open-ended, which gives the respondents an opportunity to expand on their answers, or, more usually, closed/fixed-choice questions where the respondents have limited choices.

Evaluation

+ Positivist researchers see the data collected as being highly reliable and objective.
+ There is little personal involvement on the part of the researcher after the initial construction of the questionnaire, thus reducing the risk of researcher bias.
+ Large quantities of data can be produced, and quickly and easily analysed by computer.
+ They can be used to test hypotheses, indicate social trends and make predictions of future trends.
+ They are regarded as scientific by government agencies and opinion pollsters.
+ Postal questionnaires can be sent to a sample over a wide geographical area.
− Interpretivist sociologists criticise the questionnaire for the 'imposition problem', i.e. where the researcher imposes his/her understanding on the respondent. They argue that questionnaires are not appropriate if we want to find the meanings of and motivations for social behaviour
− Different answers may not actually reflect real differences, as respondents may be interpreting questions in different ways.
− They can be too inflexible, as respondents are limited to answering only the questions asked.
− There are many problems concerning the language used and the ways in which the questions are worded.
− Operationalising concepts can involve subjectivity, as Oakley demonstrated with Young and Willmott's concept of the symmetrical family.
− Validity may be low as a result of misunderstanding, dishonesty or embarrassment.
− Postal questionnaires have their own problems, such as a low response rate, a possible lack of representativeness between those responding and the inability to check who has completed the form.
− If more qualitative data are collected, the researcher has to create categories in order to analyse them, which again involves constructs produced by the researcher.

Studies using questionnaires:

- **Peter Townsend** (1979) administered questionnaires so that he could measure the extent of poverty in the UK.
- **Shere Hite** (1988) sent out postal questionnaires to 100,000 women in the USA to question them on their sexual behaviour. Her book is based on 4,500 replies. This low response rate means that these replies cannot be taken as representative of the views of all American women.

Questionnaires for educational research

Ofsted (2007) conducted a survey of lifestyles of more than 110,000 pupils aged 10–15 years. The issues included children's fears, their attitudes to schooling, bullying, alcohol consumption, and their hopes and aspirations. The survey was completed online at participating schools.

Interviews

Several different kinds of interview are used by sociologists: structured, semi-structured and unstructured interviews; group and focus interviews, face-to-face or phone interviews. Almost all interviews involve a face-to-face interaction between an interviewer and an interviewee. They range from highly formal to a relaxed conversation. The length of the interview also varies.

- **Structured interviews**: these are pre-coded questionnaires (using an interview schedule) where standardised closed questions are asked by the interviewer to all interviewees. The quantitative data produced are easily collated and analysed by means of a computer and displayed in statistical ways to analyse patterns and trends, and to make comparisons between groups.
- **Unstructured interviews**: in contrast to the above, unstructured interviews are in-depth and non-standardised, where rapport and trust can be built up over a longer period of time. This approach is flexible, uses open-ended questions and gives the interviewees more freedom to express their views. Interpretivist and feminist researchers often adopt this qualitative method because they argue that it is a more democratic means of gaining data.
- **Semi-structured interviews**: this approach combines the advantages of both structured and unstructured interviews. The researcher can access data from standardised questions and the interviewee is able to elaborate where necessary, thus producing both quantitative and qualitative data.

Evaluation

+ Validity is likely to be high with semi-structured and unstructured interviews whereas reliability is higher with structured interviews.
+ The response rate for all interviews is much higher than for postal or self-administered questionnaires.
+ Interviewers can explain misunderstandings to the interviewee and prompt where necessary.

+ Feminists argue that unstructured interviews enable researchers to develop a more equal relationship with their subjects. Oakley used this approach with women on the labour ward in her book *From Here to Maternity*.
+ Natural settings are more likely to put interviewees at ease and help to produce more valid findings.
− Interviewer bias: the interviewer's presence will inevitably affect the interviewee. Social characteristics such as gender, ethnicity, accent etc. of the researcher will affect responses from the interviewee.
− Cost: interviews are likely to cost more than self-administered questionnaires and for this reason fewer are undertaken, making the results less representative. Unstructured interviews are more costly because they take much longer to do and the researcher has to be very skilful at encouraging the respondent to speak.
− Artificiality of the situation: the situations in which formal interviews take place are likely to reduce the validity of the data collected.
− When qualitative data are collected the researcher's own categorisation and interpretation of data may produce subjectivity. This may also reduce the validity of the data.

Studies using interviews:
● Unstructured interviews: **Dobash and Dobash** (1980) *Violence Against Wives*. The study was based on unstructured interviews with 109 women who had reported domestic violence to the police. Dobash and Dobash argued that their approach was the most appropriate because the subject matter of the research was very sensitive. They wanted to validate the women's experiences and let women speak for themselves. Their research on domestic violence led them to argue that, 'the fact is that for most people and especially women and children, the family is the most violent group to which they are likely to belong. Despite fears to the contrary it is not a stranger but a so-called loved one who is most likely to assault, rape or murder us.'
● Semi-structured interviews: **Charlotte Butler** (1995) 'Religion and gender: young women and Islam', *Sociology Review*, Vol. 4 No. 3. Butler conducted 30 semi-structured interviews with young Muslim women in Britain to discover their relationship with their faith. Her research showed that Islam was an important and positive force in their lives. Their religion gave them a strong sense of identity and her research contradicted stereotypes about the oppressive nature of religion on young Muslim women.

Interviews for educational research
● **Unstructured interviews**: **Labov (1973)** challenged the use of the formal interviews when interviewing children. In his conversations with young black boys he found that they were more forthcoming if the interviews took place less formally.

THE HENLEY COLLEGE LIBRARY

- **Group interviews**: **Willis (1977)** studied a group of working-class boys during their last year in secondary school and their first year in work. As well as participant observation, he engaged in group interviews (structured conversations) with the boys. This allowed him to observe interactions between the boys as they talked. Group interviews allow for many voices to be heard (multivocality), which according to Holstein and Gubrium (1995) broadens interviews and gives the respondents the opportunity to consider their own responses more.
- **Ball, Bowe and Gewirtz (1994)** conducted a study of 15 schools in three LEAs to examine the possible effects that parental choice and the encouragement of competition between schools had on education and on differential opportunity. They used a variety of methods including attending meetings, examining documents, visiting schools, and interviews with head teachers, parents and teachers.

Experiments: laboratory and field

The experiment is the classic research method of the natural sciences. It is the means by which hypotheses are empirically tested. Experiments involve the manipulation of an independent variable (cause) and the observation of a dependent variable (effect), while controlling extraneous variables in order to test a hypothesis.

Laboratory experiments

Laboratory experiments are designed to achieve a rigorous empirical test in which variables are closely controlled and observations and measurements are accurately recorded so that the effect of changing one or more of the variables can be analysed. By rigorous experimentation the researcher aims to identify cause and effect rather than simply a chance occurrence.

Laboratory experiments have been widely used in psychology to examine social behaviour under controlled conditions.

Evaluation

+ The experiment is internally valid if it has been conducted in a rigorous manner. It is then possible that the hypothesis has been proven, and cause and effect have been identified.
+ Through Milgram's experiment we have learned a great deal about obedience and it is possible to understand how individuals have committed atrocities under orders. Similarly, the prison simulation of Zimbardo et al. demonstrated the immediate effects of the prison on inmates and the abuse of power by the guards.
− Although experiments are the classical positivist method they have limited application in sociology. They are rarely used because of practical, theoretical and ethical reasons.

- Only a limited number of conditions can be simulated in a laboratory, making it impossible to recreate normal life.
- There is always the possibility of demand characteristics and the experimenter effect, where the awareness of being in an experiment affects the behaviour of the person undertaking the experiment.
- Many sociologists would question the ethics of conducting experiments on human beings, especially when they are being deceived about the real nature of the experiment.

Studies using experiments:

- In the 'Obedience to Authority' experiment (1974), **Stanley Milgram** found that 65% of his 40 volunteers were willing to inflict apparently dangerous electric shocks of up to 450 volts on people when instructed to do so by individuals in authority.
- **Zimbardo**'s prison study demonstrated the negative effects of allowing students to role-play prisoners and wardens.
- **Mayo** began the Hawthorne studies with an experiment to test the effects of illumination on productivity.

Field experiments

Not all experiments on people are carried out in a laboratory. Field experiments test social behaviour in the real world in everyday social contexts. For example, a study of social class conducted on Paddington Railway Station compared people's responses to a request for directions when a researcher wore a suit and bowler hat with responses to the same request when he wore clothes typical of a labourer.

Experiments for educational research

In a field experiment, **Rosenthal and Jacobson (1968)** used IQ tests to demonstrate the self-fulfilling prophecy in a primary school in California. Although now very dated, this study is still considered a classic example of teacher expectations. Many students believe this to be a participant observation study, however the researchers did not observe the classroom interactions but simply returned to the school after about a year and re-tested the pupils. This study exemplifies the fact that ethical considerations were not considered to be significant in educational research 40 years ago.

Participant observation

Participant observation involves the researcher joining the group he/she wishes to study and observing social interaction in a natural context. Participant observation is a research method commonly used by interpretivists. The researcher may observe the group with or without their knowledge.

Covert participant observation involves deception — a researcher uses a disguise or lies to the group in order to study them. With overt participant observation the group is aware they are being studied and the researcher's identity is known. However, in many participant observation studies the overt/covert line is not so clear cut because the researcher's identity may be known to some but not all of the group's members or the group may have some idea that the researcher is writing about the area/institution but not necessarily about them.

Evaluation

+ Interpretivists claim that participant observation produces highly valid data. Social actors are studied in a natural environment and the data are in-depth and detailed.
+ Unlike survey techniques the participant observer does not impose his/her definition of reality on those studied. Social actors are allowed to speak for themselves and the researcher's aim is to achieve *verstehen* — to see the world from the point of view of others.
+ Participant observation may be the only way to gain access to the group. This is likely to be the case with socially deviant groups who would not be identifiable using a traditional sampling frame.
+ Participant observation may provide answers to questions that the researcher had not even considered asking.
− Covert participant observation raises many ethical issues. The group has not given consent to being observed and their trust has been broken.
− Participant observation requires the researcher to participate in the group's activities and at the same time remain sufficiently detached to observe and interpret their behaviour. This is not an easy thing to do. Researchers can become over-involved with the group's activities, stop observing and simply take part. This is known as 'going native'. Data produced are likely to be highly biased and very subjective.
− Positivists reject this qualitative approach because they claim that it is highly unreliable and unscientific. Participant observation studies are impossible to replicate in the same way as survey data. Data produced will inevitably reflect the interests of the researcher and the way he/she interpreted events and interactions.
− Participant observation is a highly individual technique and requires tremendous skill on the part of the researcher. This is particularly true of covert participant observation where the researcher is acting all the time. Taking on the role of a member of the group may be a very stressful and dangerous experience for a sociologist involved in a group's illegal activity.
− Recording data is also difficult for covert researchers. First, they cannot risk asking too many direct questions for fear of arousing suspicion. Second, they have to find a safe and secure method of recording data. Some may resort to using hidden cameras to film their investigations. Festinger et al. made repeated visits to the toilet to write up their findings of the cult they studied. Humphreys relied on memory to write up his observations of homosexual encounters. Inevitably the sociologist will forget certain events/conversations and may interpret events in a different way from the group.
− Both joining and leaving the group can be very difficult. The researcher is likely to rely on a disguise or story to gain entry to the group and may have to leave suddenly if he/she feels under threat.

Studies using participant observation:

- **Laud Humphreys** (1970) *Tearoom Trade*. Humphreys' aim was to investigate the world of impersonal gay sexual encounters in public toilets across the USA. He wanted to show that straight men were not at risk from unwanted gay advances because they did not understand or participate in the ritual involved in gay encounters. Humphreys acted as a voyeur (look-out) for the men and repeated his observations across the USA. He wanted to discover the marital status of those men and identified them through their car registration numbers. Humphreys then visited them at home under the pretext of conducting a health survey. From the survey data he found out that many of the men were married.

- **James Patrick** (1973) *Glasgow Gang Observed*. Patrick covertly studied a gang of young men in Glasgow. He joined the gang on the invitation of one of its members, Tim, an ex-student of Patrick. He was required to take part in burglaries and observed several fights. The gang was very tough and their violence disturbed Patrick. Although he was known to Tim, he was covert to the rest of the group and he changed his appearance to fit in. Patrick's cover was almost blown on several occasions when he dressed wrongly, spoke differently and was called 'sir' by Tim out of earshot of the rest. Patrick left the group in a hurry when their violence became too problematic and he delayed publication of the study for several years using a pseudonym.
- **Sallie Westwood** (1984) *All Day Every Day: Factory and Family in the Making of Women's Lives*. This is an overt participant observation of women hosiery workers in 'Needletown'. Westwood spent a year visiting the factory and getting to know the women. She observed and interviewed women at work and joined them for nights out on the town. Her study is an illuminating account of the lives of working-class women in the Midlands, combining an ethnographic approach with a feminist analysis of marriage, relationships, family life and work.
- **Nigel Fielding** (1993) conducted covert observation of the National Front. He argued that he would not have gained access if he had been an overt observer.

Case studies

A case study is 'a detailed in-depth study of one group or event. The group or event is not necessarily representative of others of its kind, and case studies are used as preliminary pieces of research to generate hypotheses for subsequent research' (Lawson and Garrod, 1996, *The Complete A to Z Sociology Handbook*). This approach is sometimes referred to as ethnographic.

A case study may involve research into a single institution such as a school or factory, a community or even a family. The aim of a case study is to gain a detailed under-standing of the way of life of those observed. A sociologist may combine several methods in the case study but, in general, researchers tend to favour qualitative approaches such as participant observation and unstructured interviewing to gain an in-depth understanding of the group.

Evaluation

+ Case studies provide the sociologist with detailed and valid data.
+ They may serve to challenge and disprove existing assumptions about social groups. For example, the work of Eileen Barker on the Moonies challenged media fears of brainwashing by the sect.

+ The research may act as a springboard for further research in the field.
− The group or institution under study may be atypical and therefore the results will not be generalisable.
− Case studies are often a highly individual technique and this raises the problem of subjectivity on the part of the researcher.
− The data collected may be valid but are not reliable.

Studies using case studies:

- **Paul Willis**'s study *Learning to Labour* (1977) was based on 12 working-class lads and their experience of education and their first year at work.
- **Eileen Barker**'s research for *The Making of a Moonie* (1984) involved the use of surveys, unstructured interviews and participant observation over a number of years, examining recruitment patterns and the experience of life as a member of the sect.

Secondary data

Quantitative secondary data: official statistics

Official statistics are numerical data produced by both central and local government. They provide a rich source of information for sociologists.

Sociologists often differentiate between hard statistics and soft statistics. **Hard statistics** are those figures that are seen to be relatively immune to processes of manipulation and bias in their collection, e.g. birth, death, marriage and divorce statistics. Although divorce statistics may not be a particularly valid indicator of unhappiness in marriage in society, they are a completely reliable indicator of the number of divorces because you cannot legally terminate a marriage without becoming a statistic.

In contrast, **soft statistics** are those figures that are prone to subjectivity, bias and manipulation in their collection and presentation. They include data on crime, poverty, unemployment and suicide — aspects of society about which people may make value judgements. It is possible to see that the collection and interpretation of such data may be politically motivated to benefit those in power.

> **Evaluation**
>
> + Official statistics are very useful to sociologists for identifying trends and making comparisons over time and between countries.
> + Official statistics provide the sociologist with a useful source of background data. They save the sociologist vast amounts of time and expense because they are readily available.
> + Positivists see official statistics as 'hard' objective and reliable data. For example, the Census is conducted every 10 years and each household is bound by law to complete it, ensuring that the data collected are highly reliable and representative. This means that generalisations can be made about society.

- The data may not be exactly what the sociologist needs because they were collected for another purpose.
- Interpretivists question the validity of official statistics. They see them as the end product of a social process of collection.
- Figures can be subject to manipulation and bias. Marxists would argue that statistics produced by the state tend to reflect the interests of a powerful elite. They may be used to justify the existing social order.
- Feminists argue that many statistics are sexist and reflect malestream research. For example, women's social class has often been assumed to be that of their husband and women have simply been ignored in much sociological research.

Studies using official statistics:

- **Durkheim** (1897) *Le Suicide*. Durkheim's classic text *Le Suicide* was an attempt to show that society could be studied in a rigorous and scientific manner. He used nineteenth-century European statistics on suicide and compared the rate between countries. He wanted to show that suicide was not simply an individual act but a social phenomenon and had to be understood in terms of the society in which it occurred.
- **Dobash and Dobash** (1980) *Violence Against Wives*. Dobash and Dobash used crime statistics as a starting point for their research into domestic violence against women in Scotland. From the interviews they conducted, they found that many women had experienced up to 35 episodes of violence before they reported it to the police. Thus the official picture of domestic violence concealed a significant dark figure of crime.

Official statistics for educational research

There are many official statistics published annually by the Department of Education including league tables of individual schools' performance, number of qualifications by sex, ethnic group etc. These statistics are invaluable for sociological research, but the sociologist must be aware that many of them are socially constructed and, therefore, will have problems of validity and reliability.

Qualitative secondary data

Sociologists often use secondary data in their research as background sources or they may analyse secondary data to test their own hypotheses. We tend to think of secondary data as being solely statistical, but there are many other kinds of secondary material available that are qualitative, such as letters, oral histories, diaries, biographies, autobiographies, novels, newspapers, and other mass media such as film, television and photography.

Interpretivist sociologists support the use of life documents such as letters and diaries in research because individuals create these documents and reflect on their personal experiences or report their feelings about events in their lives. Interpretivist sociologists aim to achieve *verstehen* in their work and understand the meanings and motivations of social actors engaged in social action. Qualitative secondary material is in-depth, often expressive and meaningful. It should therefore enable researchers to gain a valid insight into the lives of those they wish to study.

Evaluation

+ Qualitative secondary data can be invaluable sources of information about current and historical events.
+ They may provide detailed and valid accounts of people's thoughts and feelings at a particular time.
+ Secondary data may be the only possible way of understanding a group's way of life in the past.
+ Life documents offer a richer, more in-depth picture of the way people feel and act than is possible from social surveys and other quantitative approaches.
+ The data can be usefully combined with quantitative approaches to achieve more valid and reliable findings (methodological pluralism and triangulation).
– Life documents may be highly subjective and therefore biased and invalid.
– Autobiographies are inevitably selective and partial. They were written with an audience in mind and often aim to impress the reader.
– Historical documents may not cover the particular period desired.
– Positivists reject the use of these data owing to their lack of reliability.
– As the data have to be interpreted by the researcher; this inevitably introduces the element of subjectivity.

As John Scott advises, when researchers use qualitative secondary data they should check the authenticity, credibility, meaningfulness and representativeness of them.

Studies using secondary qualitative data:

- **Thomas and Znaniecki** (1919) *The Polish Peasant in Europe and America*. The researchers made extensive use of a collection of documents including 764 letters, diaries and newspaper articles regarding immigration, and the arrival and lives of Polish émigrés in Europe and the USA.

Secondary qualitative data for educational research

Valery Hey looked at girls' friendships in two London comprehensive schools. Her study provides an interesting example of the effective use of secondary qualitative data in research. She combined overt participant observation with the use of notes scribbled in lessons and girls' diaries. The girls in her study had kept their notes and letters for several years and were willing for Hey to use them in her research. She claimed that writing notes was an important part of the girls' friendships and while teachers saw these notes as 'silliness' and 'garbage', Hey argues that 'they were socio-logically fascinating because they were an important means of transmitting the cultural values of friendship'.

Content analysis

Content analysis is the main research method used by researchers of the mass media. It can also be used to examine personal and historical documents. It is a systematic means of classifying and describing content of items in the press and on television. Content analysis can be both quantitative and qualitative depending on what the researcher is looking for.

Quantitative content analysis generates statistical data from a pre-coded coding schedule. A coding schedule is a document like a questionnaire and is completed for each newspaper article, television programme or magazine. It can be used to calculate the amount of space allocated to events and/or count the number of times a particular issue, group or even particular words occur.

Qualitative content analysis generates descriptive data and examines the messages and ideological content of the media or of particular documents. It can be used for example to look at the messages around gender or ethnic representation in the media by analysing photographs, dialogue, situations etc. This method often takes a semiological approach to texts.

Evaluation

Quantitative:

+ The material is easily available and inexpensive (even free).
+ The data are easily coded and analysed.
+ The method limits researcher effect as all coders follow the same schedule.
+ It can be used to monitor recent events and make comparisons over time.
– The problems of this method are similar to those of the questionnaire, as a coding schedule is used.
– Even though coders may be trained they may not code the material in the same way.
– Second-order constructs of the researcher may not reflect the way the audience receives the text.
– It does not address the issue of audience reception and may assume passivity.

Qualitative:

+ This method interrogates the meanings of texts and communications.
+ It can be used to interpret the underlying ideological messages of texts.
– Interpretation is a highly subjective process and individuals perceive things in different ways.
– Researchers rarely check out how the audience interprets the messages of the texts.
– Given the nature of the texts and forms of communication, the data are likely to be unrepresentative.

Studies using content analysis:

- **T.A. van Dijk** (1991) *Racism in the Press*. Van Dijk examined the coverage of race relations in the press by using both quantitative and qualitative content analysis.
- **The Glasgow Media Group** have used both quantitative and qualitative content analysis in many of their studies — from *Bad News* (1985) to *Message Received* (1999).
- This methodology has been used to look at children's literature, especially focused on gender roles.

Choice of methods (PET)

Sociologists face various decisions when conducting research. The most important one is which method(s) to choose, but this decision is also affected by many other factors. We can divide the factors that affect choice into three: practical, ethical and theoretical considerations (PET). Whichever factor is most significant depends upon the nature of the research.

Practical decisions

- **Funding**: this may be the most significant issue for any researcher. So much in research depends on the availability of money — the size of the sample, the time available for the research, the number of research assistants etc. A lone researcher may carry out a study involving participant observation where there is likely to be no external funding, but a research department may be dependent on government funding for a large social survey. Funding bodies may have ownership rights over the research data and they may have power of veto on whether the research findings can be published.
- **Time**: this is related to cost and can affect whether several interviews can take place over a period of time or if only one interview is possible.
- **Access**: without acceptance into the institution or group to be studied there will be no research. Researchers may be asked to take on a role in return for access. (For example, Willis helped with the youth wing of the school while doing his research for *Learning to Labour*.)
- **Danger**: the researcher may be placed at risk of physical harm by certain covert activities.
- **Opportunity**: the researcher needs to have research opportunities in order to undertake the research programme. Often this relies on permission being granted from those in positions of authority, such as school head teachers.

Ethical decisions

- **Moral issues**: sociologists must follow the BSA ethical guidelines. They must also be aware of the sensitivity of some areas and the possible impact of their research on respondents. Research is not usually a two-way process and respondents may feel that their trust and friendship has been betrayed. In using covert observation of any kind, the subjects are always deceived.
- **Illegality**: researchers may be called upon to engage in criminal acts or to witness others doing so.
- **Danger**: in some cases researchers may place their subjects in danger during their study.

- **After-effects**: some methods such as experimentation may have short-term or more lasting effects on respondents who might have been misinformed about the nature of the study.
- **Informed consent**: the researcher should try to conduct the research with the consent of the subjects. This gives them the opportunity to refuse to participate or to withdraw at any time.

Theoretical decisions

- The methodological approach of the researcher is likely to affect the choice of method. Positivists generally choose quantitative methods.
- The theoretical perspective of the researcher — whether he/she is Marxist, interpretivist, feminist etc — will affect choice of method and the nature of the research.

The application of research methods to the study of education

Sociologists studying the topic of education will choose methods that they find most appropriate and this, in effect, means that all sociological research methods are available to them. The choice of method depends on practical, ethical and theoretical factors, including the topics and issues to be investigated and the individuals to be researched.

One practical issue with researching children is that the younger the children, the less likely they will be able to complete lengthy questionnaires.

An important ethical issue is that of consent, as researchers must gain consent not only from the school but also from parents and guardians. It is most important to ensure that children are not harmed or disadvantaged in any way as a result of the research.

Questions & Answers

This section of the guide contains four papers on **Education and Sociological Methods** in the style of the AQA unit examination. The first three papers include both grade C and grade A responses to each question. It is important to note that grade A responses are not 'model answers'. They do not represent the only, or even necessarily the best, way of answering these questions. It would be quite possible — particularly in the essay-type questions — to take a different approach, to use different material or even to come to a different conclusion, and still gain very high marks. Rather, the responses represent a particular 'style' in answering the question set while displaying the appropriate skills, including the use of appropriate concepts and studies. They also demonstrate a critical and evaluative awareness towards the material used, and present a logically structured argument. Grade C responses may be on the right track but fail, for various reasons, to score as many marks. A fourth paper is provided without candidates' responses. This is for you to answer and some tips are provided to help you.

We have not been able to produce responses so that whole papers are given A or C grades. As the examination papers have several sections, it would be entirely possible for a candidate to achieve high marks on one section and low marks on others. This means that there are different routes to achieving particular grades.

The candidate responses are accompanied by examiner's comments. These are preceded by the icon 𝒆 and indicate where credit is due. For the grade A answers, the examiner points out the factors that enable the candidates to score so highly. Particular attention is given to the candidates' use of the examinable skills: knowledge and understanding, application and analysis, and evaluation. For the grade C answers, the examiner points out areas for improvement, specific problems and common errors.

Total for this paper: 90 marks

Question 1

Read Item A below and answer parts (a) to (d) that follow.

Item A

Sociologists of education have competing theories relating to the role that the education system plays in wider society. Some structural theorists look at education as responding to the needs of the society. This may be in terms of the functions it performs to maintain and perpetuate society, or its role in reproducing social inequality. Some sociologists see education as part of a meritocratic society, whereas others argue that processes within schools such as the hidden curriculum maintain an unequal society.

(a) **Explain what is meant by the term 'hidden curriculum'.** (2 marks)

(b) **Suggest *three* policies that government or educational bodies have introduced to overcome what is seen as some pupils' cultural deprivation.** (6 marks)

(c) **Outline some of the reasons for the existence of anti-school subcultures.** (12 marks)

(d) **Using material from Item A and elsewhere, assess the view that the modern education system is a meritocracy.** (20 marks)

Total: 40 marks

Answer to question 1: grade C candidate

(a) Things like obedience to authority that schools teach pupils.

> The candidate has given an example rather than a definition of the term and scores only 1 mark out of the 2 available.

(b) Sending parents to classes to help their children to read.

> The candidate has given only one possible policy here, but it is correct and scores 2 out of 6 marks. Always check carefully that you have followed the instructions in the question.

(c) Willis studied one anti-school subculture. They were called the 'lads'. They were not interested in school but wanted to have a 'laff'. They spent their time messing around in school and wasting teachers' time. What they valued was manual work. The other groups were called the 'ear'oles' because they listened to the teachers and wanted to get qualifications. Willis said that education was really just preparation for working-class jobs and the lads were getting used to being bored at work.

Hargreaves went into school as a teacher and watched how the boys behaved in class. He found that many boys in the lower stream messed about and did not do well in school. The teachers did not expect them to do well and this caused a self-fulfilling prophecy.

Sometimes pupils are bored in school and gang up to cause trouble.

> The candidate has shown some reasonable knowledge, but there is little analysis as the points are merely described. There is no explicit evaluation. The candidate does not focus on the *reasons* for the existence of anti-school subcultures. Remember the importance of reading the question carefully and then doing what it asks you to do. This response gains 6 out of 12 marks.

(d) Marxists and functionalists see the education system in very different ways. Functionalists like Parsons and Durkheim see education as a meritocracy. This means that everyone has the same chance of succeeding in school. Education teaches the next generation the skills necessary for work. Functionalists believe that society must be kept stable and in balance and that education is important in helping society to achieve social order. They say that everyone must have shared norms and values in order for the system to work.

> This is a reasonable opening paragraph. There are links made between functionalism and ideas of meritocracy, but the candidate does not demonstrate the ways in which education can make this happen.

But Marxists disagree. They see education as a tool of the bourgeoisie to keep the working classes down. In school, children learn to be obedient and respect teachers. The system isn't fair for working-class children because they fail and as one sociologist said school teaches working-class boys how to get working-class jobs. The lads in his study did not try to succeed in school and formed their own deviant subculture.

Bowles and Gintis said that the school system corresponded to capitalism and pupils are exploited by teachers. Capitalism needs workers who have been brain-washed to accept the power of the bourgeoisie. This happens through the hidden curriculum.

> Again the candidate shows some reasonable knowledge and understanding of theory. Evaluation is presented by juxtaposing Marxism and functionalism.

In conclusion, functionalists and Marxists disagree about the role of education. However, from my understanding most sociologists would reject the idea that education is fair for everyone because working-class children and boys tend to underachieve in school.

> There is more evaluation here even though it is limited.

> **Overall, the answer demonstrates potentially relevant material that really needs to be developed to gain higher marks. However, the candidate fails**

to make any explicit reference to the material in Item A. This is significant, as failure to make any reference to the item would prevent the candidate scoring higher marks. If the question states 'with reference to the item and elsewhere', failure to do so means that you have not answered what is asked of you. This candidate gains 13 out of 20 marks.

Answer to question 1: grade A candidate

(a) This refers to things outside the official curriculum that pupils are taught, like discipline, obedience to authority, all the values and beliefs; it can even mean sexism and racism.

  This is a competent definition and also includes appropriate examples. It gains 2 out of 2 marks. It is often useful to include a relevant example, though this is not essential unless the question asks for it.

(b) There are many policies that do this. They include:
- Operation Headstart in the USA
- SureStart in Britain
- Saturday schools
- Educational Action Zones

  This candidate gives more responses than are asked for, but they are all correct. Even if one of the responses were incorrect, the candidate would score full marks for the three correct ones. The candidate scores 6 out of 6 marks.

(c) Sociologists have identified several reasons for the existence of anti-school subcultures. These are the effects of setting and streaming, labelling, laddism and resistance.

Hargreaves carried out the earliest work into anti-school subcultures. He showed that labelling boys and placing them in lower streams created anti-school feelings. Not only did the boys feel that they didn't count in school but their teachers treated them differently from the top stream. More recently, one of Peter Woods' pupil adaptations was rebellion where pupils rejected the means and goals of educational success.

This reflects the behaviour of Willis' lads in *Learning to Labour*. Their anti school subculture was mainly about having a 'laff'. They experienced school as alienating and as a result created an anti-school subculture as a coping strategy. Although he argued that these working-class lads were able to see through the system, it still operated to reproduce the class system.

Gillborn's work showed that teachers' attitudes towards black boys as 'troublemakers' led to anti-school resistance and challenge from these boys.

Finally, feminists criticise male stream research which has ignored girls and anti-school subcultures.

✎ The candidate shows good knowledge and understanding focused on the question. He/she has been successful in interpreting, applying, analysing and evaluating the material. The candidate scores the full 12 out of 12 marks.

(d) A meritocracy means a fair system where pupils will achieve success on the basis of their own efforts and ability. This view sees education as a system where the most talented and hard working will succeed.

✎ This is a good, clear introduction. The candidate demonstrates good knowledge and understanding of the concept.

According to Item A, structural theorists have competing views as to whether education is meritocratic. The view held by functionalists is that the education system performs an essential role in the selection process of people into appropriate roles in the economy. Parsons and Davis and Moore all saw education as meritocratic. They argue that individuals are not born intellectually equal. Intelligence is genetic and the role of the education system is to select the most able for the most functionally important roles in society. Therefore, doctors and lawyers are naturally more intelligent than cleaners and porters. In Parsons' view a meritocratic education system was essential in a modern society. He saw the education system as a bridge between home and work. In the family, individuals are judged on 'particularistic' values; however, the education system, like the world of work, is based on 'universalistic' values.

✎ This paragraph develops the acceptance of a meritocracy from the functionalist perspective. The candidate demonstrates an effective use of relevant examples and understands the relationship between home, school and work. There is a useful reference to Item A.

However, not all functionalists shared this view. Melvin Tumin said that Davis and Moore's work was too simplistic because there was no way of measuring the functional importance of particular jobs.

✎ This short paragraph begins to evaluate the argument.

Other structural theorists like Marxists see education as 'reproducing social inequality' (Item A) and reject the view that education is a meritocracy. They see that education really functions in the interest of the ruling class. Althusser saw education as an Ideological State Apparatus, which legitimates class inequality in society. Bowles and Gintis showed that there was a correspondence between the education system and the economy. The economy 'cast a long shadow over education'. This means that schools exert ideological control and are moulded according to the needs of capitalism. Through the hidden curriculum children learn to be obedient and to respect authority. Relationships between teachers and students are said to mirror those of employers and employees.

✎ This paragraph demonstrates sophisticated knowledge. The paragraph is both evaluative and analytical. The candidate is challenging the functionalist viewpoint by using the Marxist critique effectively. Good use is made of Item A again.

Willis did an ethnographic study on 12 working-class boys where he showed that the boys could see through the system even though it meant that they still ended up with working-class jobs. He argued that the education system prepared working-class kids for working-class jobs.

A recent report by the Rowntree Trust showed that far from there being greater equality in society, children — especially boys — from poorer backgrounds, were doing even worse than before. This clearly shows that the functionalists were wrong in their views. Recent evidence also shows that increasing numbers of successful professionals like lawyers, MPs, judges etc. generally come from Oxbridge and top public schools.

e This paragraph makes good use of the item to show that a pupil's background has an important part to play in success, thus challenging the view that the modern education system is a meritocracy.

In conclusion we can see that the system is a long way from being meritocratic and still today the wealthier your background, the more likely you are to succeed.

e **Overall this candidate has demonstrated excellent sociological knowledge and understanding and has a sophisticated grasp of criticisms. The essay is sophisticated and coherent and the candidate scores full marks, 20 out of 20.**

Question 2

This question requires you to apply your knowledge and understanding of socio-logical research methods to the study of this particular issue in education.

Read Item B and answer the question that follows.

Item B

Gender and classroom relationships

From the 1970s feminist researchers in education have shown us that boys seeking the attention of their teachers dominated classrooms. It wasn't that teachers were consciously ignoring the girls; rather the space was more often taken over by the boys. It is interesting to note that this did not necessarily prevent the progress of the girls. Other factors were affecting their aspirations and achievements, for example subject channelling, careers advice and parental expectations.

Most classroom research has been qualitative and primary, undertaken by inter-pretivists and feminists. However, other more recent research has focused upon the usefulness of secondary data.

Using material from Item B and elsewhere, assess the strengths and limitations of *one* of the following methods for the study of gender and classroom relationships:

(i) Primary methods
(ii) Secondary data   20 marks

Answer to question 2: grade C candidate

(i) Item B says that most research was primary and qualitative. This means that the researchers did it themselves. Many researchers used participant observation (PO) to find out what was really happening in the classroom. Hargreaves became a teacher to look at the classroom but this did not really work and he then told the teachers he was a researcher. He found out things like how streaming and labelling were important influences on the boys' progress, but he only looked at boys.

> The candidate begins well by correctly identifying an appropriate primary method, but Hargreaves' study is not well focused on the issue of gender and classroom relationships.

Feminists like Dale Spender say that the classroom is male dominated. Her methods have been criticised because she was teaching and researching in the classroom at the same time, but this is really impossible to do.

> This is useful material, but needs further development. The candidate might have explained how the research was conducted in more detail. There might be advantages to this kind of research as well as disadvantages.

Stanworth did interviews with teachers in secondary schools. She found that male teachers hardly knew the girls in their classes and assumed they would become secretaries. However, she did not actually watch what went on in the classroom, so this has problems.

> This paragraph contains more relevant material and the candidate makes a useful criticism of the research. Again it could be more developed.

In conclusion, many sociologists use triangulation in their research. This makes for more validity and reliability.

> This could have been a reasoned conclusion if the candidate had explained how triangulation enhanced validity and reliability. By linking the concepts we can only assume that the candidate does not know the differences between them.

> **The essay could be improved by reference to other primary methods such as quantitative ones. The range of methods here is quite narrow, but relevant research is stated. However, there is no mention of the theoretical context of the various methods and little made of practical or ethical considerations. There is also limited analysis and evaluation. The candidate scores 11 out of 20 marks.**

Answer to question 2: grade A candidate

(ii) Secondary data include all those things collected by other people for different purposes. They can be quantitative and qualitative and both positivists and interpretivists can use them. In terms of gender and classroom relationships the types of data could include: classroom notes such as those Valery Hey used, educational statistics on gender and achievement, possibly people's own written accounts of their personal experience of classrooms, and other sociologists' previous research.

🖉 This is a very coherent introduction. The candidate has made reference to theory and to the varieties of secondary data that may be available to use.

According to Item B, early feminist research showed that boys dominated the classroom. As sociologists we can use the results of Spender and Stanworth who researched this area but used primary data. This is useful as secondary data because we can use the data historically as it is over 30 years since it was collected. It can be useful to use comparatively and to measure social changes that might have taken place. We also know how they did their methodology and we can learn from possible mistakes. This would be true of any other primary research that was conducted on gender relations in classrooms. There have been several studies into gender in the primary classroom and we can see how gender affects the classroom at different educational stages. This would be useful to show educational policy makers.

🖉 This is a sophisticated paragraph. At first glance the essay may appear to be quite challenging, but this candidate has seen how useful the work of previous sociologists could be in this field. Reference is also made to Item B.

Valery Hey actually used secondary sources in her gender research. Although she did not focus specifically on classroom relationships, it might be possible to ask students to keep their own records of what happens in classrooms in relation to who gets most attention. Interpretivists would like this research as it gives insight into personal meanings of situations. On the other hand, educational statistics, liked by positivists, might give more insight into gender differences between single-sex and mixed-sex classrooms.

In conclusion, secondary data can be used in a variety of ways to understand this topic. Perhaps the most useful way of gaining a thorough understanding would be to combine secondary data with some primary research. This would give us more valid insight because we would get closer to the reality of the situation and more positivistic methods would produce more reliability.

🖉 **Overall this is a very sophisticated response to this question. The candidate has identified strengths and limitations of secondary data and has linked methods to theoretical contexts. Relevant research has also been incorporated. It would be difficult to do better under examination conditions. The candidate scores full marks, 20 out of 20.**

Question 3

This question permits you to draw examples from any areas of sociology with which you are familiar.

(a) Explain what is meant by the term 'validity'. (2 marks)

(b) Suggest two reasons why some sociologists choose to use snowball sampling. (4 marks)

(c) Suggest two reasons why sociologists wish their samples to be representative. (4 marks)

(d) Examine the reasons why some sociologists prefer to use participant observation in their research. (20 marks)

Total: **30 marks**

Answer to question 3: grade C candidate

(a) This is whether the data are accurate.

> ✏ This is too vague to score any marks. 'Accuracy' is not a sufficient definition without more clarification.

(b) You can't find enough people by yourself. Laurie Taylor used one.

> ✏ There is only one partially correct answer here. The reference to Laurie Taylor does not tell us when or why he used the technique. The candidate only gains 1 out of 4 marks.

(c) So they can generalise their data to reveal information about the whole research population.

They want their findings to be valid.

> ✏ The first response here is appropriate, but the second is incorrect. The candidate scores 2 marks out of 4.

(d) Some sociologists like interpretivists use participant observation in their research. They argue that it gives them meanings and motivations.

There are two types of participant observation, covert and overt. James Patrick used covert participant observation in his study of a Glasgow gang because he wanted to find out what it was really like inside a gang. He couldn't have given the gang questionnaires to fill in because they would have refused and they were very aggressive.

> ✏ This is a reasonable introduction. The candidate has correctly identified two main types of participant observation, but hasn't yet explained the differences between them.

Laud Humphreys also used covert participant observation in *Tearoom Trade*. He became a 'watch queen' for men having sex in public toilets. He did not take part, but he was still covert because they did not know that he was researching them. He had to write up notes in the car. Many sociologists have criticised this study because it was unethical.

What Humphreys did next was to take down the registration numbers of the men's cars and his friend who was in the police gave him their names and addresses. He then included these men in his health questionnaire to find out if they were married or not. This is very unethical because he knew things about them from the participant observation. The advantages of his study were that he found out that some of the men were married and went home to wives and families. This showed that not all married men were 'straight' and he couldn't have done the study if he hadn't used covert participant observation.

e This is a rather lengthy description of one study. Material has been interpreted accurately, but the candidate has still not focused on the 'reasons' for the use of the method.

There is also overt participant observation but this gives the Hawthorne effect because people know that they are being studied and they act differently. This makes the data invalid.

In conclusion, positivists do not use participant observation because they see it as unreliable and unscientific. They prefer quantitative methods like structured interviews and questionnaires in their research.

e This is a brief but reasonable conclusion.

e **The candidate has missed opportunities to focus on the reasons for the use of participant observation even though he/she has a reasonable knowledge and understanding of the method. It is very important to be clear what the question is asking you to do. This response scores 12 out of 20.**

Answer to question 3: grade A candidate

(a) Validity means if the data measure what the researcher set out to measure. It means whether the data are close to the reality of the social situation.

e This is a clear definition and scores the full 2 marks.

(b) There is no sampling frame and the samples are hard to access. They are often in deviant or secret groups.

e The candidate has produced four possible correct responses here. Any two will count (4 out of 4 marks).

(c) If the funding body is the government it wants to make sure that it can talk about the wider population.

By having a representative sample sociologists are aiming to avoid distortion/bias because the sample is a good cross section of the target population.

So they don't have an atypical sample.

> 🖉 The candidate has produced more than two appropriate reasons and would score full marks for any two — 4 out of 4 marks.

(d) Participant observation is a qualitative method used by interpretivists. It allows the researcher to study a group in order to gain in-depth understanding of what it is like to be a member of such a group. It can be either overt where the group being studied are aware of the researcher's presence and aims; or covert where the researcher's identity is hidden from the group. Covert participant observation is a very popular method for studying deviant and secret groups because it allows the observer to get inside the group without the members knowing that they are being researched. It is also considered to be the method that produces the most valid data as it is as close as a researcher can get to the meanings of social action and the reasons why such action takes place.

> 🖉 This is a clear and coherent introduction. The candidate has put the method into a theoretical context and has started to look at reasons for its use.

Sociologists choose covert participant observation because it has many advantages for them. It gives them access to groups not otherwise available, especially groups who would not respond to questionnaires or structured interviews. For example, both Patrick and Humphreys used covert participant observation to study hard-to-access groups. This enabled them to understand and see from the inside what the lives of these people were really like.

> 🖉 This is a very useful paragraph. It identifies a reason clearly and uses supporting evidence in a concise and relevant manner. The candidate avoids the pitfall of lengthy descriptions.

Goffman also found that being covert in an American mental hospital enabled him to see processes at work that even the staff weren't aware of, such as 'making out'.

Another important reason for using covert participant observation was shown by William Foote Whyte. He used an informer to gain access to his research group. Although there were problems with his research, he showed the importance of standing back and listening. He said 'I learned answers to questions I hadn't thought of asking'. So he wouldn't have gained the same kind of information if he had used questionnaires or structured interviews. The major problem was that he changed Doc's role in the group by using him as a key informant. Doc said, 'You slowed me up plenty, Bill' because Doc became an observer as well.

> 🖉 This is another well-focused paragraph that identifies another appropriate reason for participant observation. It contains contrast evaluation and makes a useful evaluative point on a disadvantage.

However, there are many reasons as to why researchers would choose overt over covert participant observation. If the researcher is being truthful with the group members they are more likely to trust the researcher and build a rapport with them. This will produce more in-depth, valid data and the researcher will gain greater insight into their actions. It solves the problem of deception and prevents any possible danger of illegality, as the researcher would not feel pressured into getting too involved. However, unlike covert participant observation, it produces the Hawthorne effect and this might challenge the validity of the data. On the other hand it allows the researcher to record events openly rather than having to rely on retrospective memory. In some cases, even though it is not respected by the ethics of the BSA, covert participant observation might be the only method that allows a researcher to gain valuable insights, such as Fielding in his study of a right-wing political group.

Eileen Barker justified her overt research into the Moonies by saying that she did not want to deceive the members. Although they were wary of her at first, she soon became a trusted stranger and many of them confided in her. She spent several years visiting the movement and gained insights that would not have been available from other methods.

e These studies are well applied and the candidate solves the limitations of one kind of participant observation by using them as strengths of the other.

In conclusion, interpretivists see that this method is very useful in gaining in-depth, qualitative and valid data. However, positivists would criticise it as unreliable and unrepresentative.

e This is a brief but reasoned conclusion.

e **The essay demonstrates a range of reasons. It is conceptually detailed and well focused on reasons. There is some slight imbalance as most of the studies are covert and less is made of the overt dimension. However, it still gains a top band mark of 18 out of 20.**

NB It is very important when answering a question that asks for 'reasons' that you don't take the advantages versus disadvantages approach. This would cost you valuable time and marks, as it does not answer the question set.

aper 2

Total for this paper: 90 marks

Question 1

Read Item A below and answer parts (a) to (d) that follow.

Item A

Some of the main causes of the underachievement of some ethnic minority students relate to factors within the school. Negative labelling and stereotypical assumptions by teachers can often result in some ethnic minority students acting up to their label. There is some evidence to show that the gap between success and failure between some ethnic groups is widening rather than narrowing. However social class and gender are also very significant factors that cut across ethnicity. Indeed some schools may be seen to operate a gender regime.

(a) **Explain what is meant by the term 'gender regime'.** (2 marks)
(b) **Suggest *three* aspects of the hidden curriculum.** (6 marks)
(c) **Outline some of the reasons why females now achieve higher results than males in the education system.** (12 marks)
(d) **Using material from Item A and elsewhere, assess sociological explanations of the differential educational achievement of ethnic groups.** (20 marks)

Total: 40 marks

Answer to question 1: grade C candidate

(a) This is where girls and boys are separated into different subjects like girls into netball and boys into football.

> 🖉 This a relatively simplistic definition, but the candidate has some limited awareness of gender selection. He/she gains 1 mark out of 2 for a partial explanation.

(b) The hidden curriculum is a Marxist term that shows that schools are part of the capitalist system. It is all those things that are not taught officially and you can't really explain how it happens, but pupils learn to obey teachers.

> 🖉 The candidate has some understanding of the term, but has not provided three different aspects. However, 'pupils learn to obey teachers' gains 2 out of 6 marks.

(c) Since the introduction of the National Curriculum, girls have become much more successful than boys at GCSE. Since 1990 there has been a 10% gap between boys and girls. Here are some of the reasons why girls are more successful:

The introduction of coursework since the 1980s has helped girls achieve higher grades, as they tend to be more consistent than boys over the year and boys tend to put more effort in just before the exams.

The changing position of women in society (economic independence and lone-parent mothers) has shown girls the importance of having a career. So they have become more career-minded now than in the 1970s. Sue Sharpe showed that girls' priorities in the 1970s and the 1990s were different. Although she found that in the 1970s girls mainly wanted to get married and have a family, in the 1990s girls wanted a career first.

The National Curriculum means that boys and girls have to study core subjects like science and maths and so girls have not been able to drop science, and have done well at it.

Parents' attitudes have also changed. They now encourage their daughters to do well, not just to get married. So we can see that all these things work together to put girls ahead of boys.

> The candidate gives several reasons for the achievement of girls. There is good knowledge and understanding and interpretation is well focused. There is some explicit evaluation — **8 out of 12 marks.**

(d) There are several reasons that sociologists put forward to explain the under-achievement of ethnic minority groups. First, schools and teachers have been accused of being racist.

> Many candidates assume that pupils from all ethnic minorities underachieve. It appears this candidate is going to do this.

Bernard Coard said that the British education system made the black child educationally subnormal. Teachers treat black boys as troublemakers and often see them as aggressive and as a threat in the classroom. Jayleigh School is an example of a school that was racist. In the school, streaming was closely linked to race. Asian students were placed in lower streams and so they were not entered for as many GCSEs as white students. Since this study, Jayleigh has changed its attitudes.

> Here the candidate has differentiated between groups of students, if only implicitly, by examining the positions of black boys and Asian pupils. It is always helpful to identify the author(s) of any study referred to, if this is known.

According to Cecile Wright, ethnic minority pupils in primary school were treated differently from white pupils. Asian pupils were ignored by teachers who thought that they could not speak English. Black boys were treated unfairly. They were expected to behave badly and were punished by the teacher. Black pupils are much more likely to be permanently excluded from school compared with white pupils. This is due to the racism of many teachers. Other sociologists have seen language and home background as important factors and some parents have set up black-only schools.

paper

 There is some reasonable knowledge and understanding here. However, there is a lack of balanced argument in the response as the candidate assumes that there are no differences between the groups. In order to address the question more competently, he/she should have referred to the high achievement of groups such as Chinese and African students. There is no reference made to Item A and the essay lacks a conclusion. The response scores 8 out of 20 marks.

Answer to question 1: grade A candidate

(a) This is difficult to describe. It's a school run on gender lines. Usually patriarchy dominates, the hierarchy is male and there are sexist attitudes in the school that aren't challenged by staff.

 This is a good attempt at a difficult concept. The candidate has a notion of a ruling system and one that favours one gender over the other. The answer gains 2 out of 2 marks.

(b) The hidden curriculum includes a range of aspects. Because there is fragmentation of knowledge where the curriculum is split into different subjects and times of day, pupils don't have any power over timing and what they learn.

They have to be punctual and learn to be disciplined. It also includes gender social-isation and even how to learn to accept boredom.

 This is a sophisticated response and includes at least six different and relevant aspects. However, it is important not to get carried away and write very full responses to this question, as timing is important. The candidate gains 2 marks for each of three correct aspects — 6 out of 6 marks.

(c) Since the 1990s there has been a consistent gap between the achievement of boys and girls. Girls now outperform boys by at least 10% at GCSE and the gap has closed at A-level too. One reason identified for girls' success has been changing parental attitudes. Parents are now placing more emphasis on their daughters' education. They have higher expectations of their daughters throughout their school lives.

There is evidence that in the past girls did not underachieve but the dice was loaded against them. Under the tripartite system, girls generally achieved higher 11+ scores than boys but allocation to grammar schools was unfair. This may be an indication that girls have not suddenly outperformed boys in education, but that overall factors in wider society, including sexist attitudes towards women, had not given them equal opportunities.

Sue Sharpe claimed that girls in the 1970s placed little emphasis on educational success. However, two decades later she found that girls had changed their attitudes to educational achievement and wanted a career.

New policies in education (e.g. GIST and WISE) and the National Curriculum resulted in a greater achievement of girls. Girls now study what were traditionally seen as 'male' areas and they have been very successful. There are many other reasons for girls' achievement. Feminists would argue that raised awareness of women's social position and wider social changes in the family, such as more lone-parent families headed by women and more women employed in professional and managerial roles in the labour market have been very significant.

> ✍ This candidate has shown good knowledge and understanding and has been successful in interpreting, applying, analysing and evaluating material relevant to the question. This answer gains the full 12 marks.

(d) It is important to say at the beginning of this essay that ethnic minority groups do not all perform the same in education. In fact, the highest achieving groups include groups such as Chinese, Indian and some African students, whereas in the lowest achieving groups there are Afro-Caribbean, Bangladeshi and Turkish students. An interesting fact is that the group at the bottom of the achievement ladder is white working-class boys.

> ✍ This is an impressive start. The candidate is aware that 'ethnic minority' groups do not constitute a homogeneous category and has included some examples of differential educational achievement to illustrate this.

Many early sociological explanations focused on cultural and language factors as the causes of underachievement. More recently, however, the focus has widened to include what happens in school as well as racism more generally.

> ✍ This candidate clearly understands that this is a complex question and demonstrates that explanations have changed over time. Evaluation is explicit here.

In the past, language barriers were identified as a major cause of underachievement for students where English was not the main language spoken at home. However, Ballard and Driver's research showed that language difficulties were no longer an issue by the time the student reached 16. These students of this age were as fluent in English as their classmates. Today most sociologists would reject language factors as the major cause of underachievement.

> ✍ In this paragraph, the candidate both identifies and analyses the issue of language effectively. It is evaluative and the candidate makes reference to appropriate research.

Cultural deprivation was also blamed for the underachievement of some groups. For example, in his study Ken Pryce suggested that Afro-Caribbean families were 'turbulent', lacking a 'sense of close dependence on each other'. It was argued that these families did not provide adequate cultural capital for their children. Some sociologists and politicians saw the higher proportion of lone-parent families within this group as yet another reason for their relative failure.

> ✍ Both of these paragraphs provide material relevant to the argument that underachievement in education is related to home factors. This should now be balanced by evidence of in-school factors.

However, the Swann Report challenged many of these stereotypical views and indicated that if class were not a factor, these students would not be disadvantaged. Indeed, the report claimed that low social class accounted for at least 80% of educational underachievement.

Social class was more significant for specific ethnic minority groups, such as those from Bangladesh and Pakistan and some Afro-Caribbean students, as these groups are disproportionately working class. Therefore issues such as material deprivation may also play a significant role.

Other arguments blamed the education system itself. Bernard Coard's research is particularly significant in examining disadvantage. Although dated, his work shows that black pupils were made to feel 'educationally subnormal' for four main reasons: the idea that their language is second-rate and unacceptable in class; the association of 'white' with 'good' and 'black' with 'bad' in children's literature; poor and stereotypical representation of ethnic minorities in school textbooks; and racism from other students. Coard concludes that this inevitably led to the self-fulfilling prophecy of underachievement. In 1999, Ofsted identified the British education system as institutionally racist in terms of its curriculum and personnel.

Further evidence came from the Jayleigh study which showed that within inner-city schools, ethnic minority pupils were at a disadvantage in terms of GCSE entries, being in lower sets and having to achieve higher grades in order to be perceived as successful. Wright's study found that some ethnic minority groups received poorer interaction from staff. Teachers' perceptions were seen as stereotypical; although Asian students were seen as 'good', black students were seen as disruptive and disobedient.

🖉 The candidate now takes up the alternative, critical positions, looking at factors pointing to institutional racism.

In conclusion, it is clear that this is a complex issue. Some of the highest achieving groups are from ethnic minorities. We also need to take into account that we cannot separate ethnicity from social class and gender. Research on interaction between staff and students, including studies such as Fuller's and Mac an Ghaill's has shown that pupils can resist negative labels and teacher expectations.

🖉 **This is a very sophisticated response that demonstrates high-level knowledge and understanding of arguments and evidence and the essential skills of evaluation and analysis. Overall, this is an excellent response and worthy of 20 out of 20 marks.**

Question 2

This question requires you to apply your knowledge and understanding of sociological research methods to the study of this particular issue in education.

Read Item B and answer the question that follows.

Item B

The hidden curriculum includes all those things that students learn within the school environment that are not 'officially' taught. According to Marxists, the organisation of the school, teacher/pupil relationships, the importance of competition and individualism and even the decisions as to what is included within subjects can all be seen as part of the hidden curriculum.

For example, within schools there is a hierarchy of authority. Students learn to obey this authority and it is used to enforce discipline. Many sociologists would agree that the hidden curriculum has a significant impact on a student's experience of education and also on their likelihood of educational success or failure.

Using material from Item B and elsewhere, assess the strengths and limitations of one of the following methods for studying some aspects of the hidden curriculum on pupils:

(i) Structured interviews
(ii) Classroom observation   **20 marks**

Answer to question 2: grade C candidate

(i) According to Item B, the hidden curriculum includes authority and obedience and discipline. Marxists say that it's very important but it is difficult to find out about it. Positivists like structured interviews because they are quantitative and reliable but interpretivists say that they are not valid.

> 🖉 The candidate introduces the essay with reference to Item B. This is usually a good strategy, as many students forget to make any reference to the item. However, in this case, the candidate has not used the item, but simply stated it.

There are two main types of interview. Unstructured interviews are more like conversations and they do not have pre-set schedules of questions. Structured interviews are like spoken questionnaires. There is a pre-set schedule of questions that are asked of all interviewees in exactly the same way. Their advantage is that they are easy to analyse and make correlations, and positivists like Durkheim say that you can identify social laws from them.

> 🖉 This is sound knowledge and understanding and the points are developed. In any essay on research methods, it is very important to introduce the theoretical context. There is also some evaluation here. Note that there is, as yet, no reference to interviews in the context of the hidden curriculum.

However, interpretivists say that they are not valid, because they do not provide depth or meaning behind the questions. They would prefer unstructured interviews, because the interviewee is able to talk as if they were in a conversation and you get more valid data.

☑ This is the opposing view. It challenges structured interviews and gives an appropriate concept. Again, so far the comments about the two types of interview are general ones, not specific to the question set.

In school it is better to use structured interviews, because children will not want to give long answers to someone that they do not know. Mac an Ghaill used unstructured interviews when he was asking boys questions about masculinity. Michelle Stanworth used structured interviews when she researched gender in the classroom. She found that some teachers did not know the names of girls in their class. This shows part of the hidden curriculum because gender and ethnicity are part of the hidden curriculum. However, she would have found more in-depth data if she had done some classroom observation.

☑ This paragraph places the method in the context of schooling. It is important that this is done, as the question relates to 'methods in context'. The studies are applied to the method, even if they are not completely correct. The candidate also refers to the hidden curriculum, again a reference to the Item. There is a limited attempt at contrast evaluation in the comparison of structured interviews and classroom observation.

In conclusion, structured interviews can be useful, but researchers would get reliable and valid data if they used semi-structured interviews.

☑ It is unfortunate that the candidate has conflated validity and reliability here and does not gain marks for these concepts. There is an attempt at a conclusion, but the candidate has introduced another form of interview that does not appear earlier in the essay and the point is not developed.

☑ **Overall, the essay is not well focused on the question, but there is some theory and some appropriate knowledge and understanding. The candidate gains 13 out of 20 marks.**

Answer to question 2: grade A candidate

(ii) According to Item B, the hidden curriculum is extremely important within schools. It is also very widespread, as we can see that it includes organisation, competition, individualism and discipline. This makes it difficult to research its impact. One aspect of the hidden curriculum is that of teacher/pupil relationships, and the method I have chosen is classroom observation.

☑ This is a very good start. We are introduced to the topic of the hidden curriculum; reference is made to Item B and to the chosen method.

One of the first sociologists to use classroom observation was Hargreaves. He was interested in the process by which teachers got to know their students. He argued that there were three stages to this process: speculation, elaboration and stabilisation. He watched this process at work within classrooms.

☑ This is sound knowledge and understanding. There is some development of Hargreaves' work and it is clearly related to the question.

At first, teachers created an image of a student or of a class based on limited knowledge and guesses. This was followed with a hypothesis using more evidence of the student/class, based on likeability, enthusiasm, deviancy etc. and finally, this hypothesis was confirmed and the student/class was treated as if they were actually like this. All future teacher/pupil interactions were based on this view. Hargreaves was able to follow this process by being in the classrooms and watching it take place. He could not have gained this kind of data with structured questionnaires, as teachers — even if they recognised the process — would not admit to doing it themselves.

🖉 Although the candidate begins in a descriptive way, he/she develops the point with an example and then includes some contrast evaluation in the form of structured questionnaires.

Spender's work also shows an aspect of the hidden curriculum in the classroom, but this time in relation to gender. From observations of her own classes, she discovered that boys dominated the classroom. Even though she was a feminist, she was surprised to find that she, herself, gave boys more attention than she gave the girls. Again her work shows us how useful classroom observation is, but she has been criticised for not being objective. It is difficult to teach and observe at the same time and it might make her work invalid.

🖉 Another study applied well here. Spender is used to show another aspect of the hidden curriculum, but within the context of teacher/pupil relationships. There is relevant evaluation here, highlighting the problem of teachers researching their own classrooms. 'Invalid' is an appropriate concept in this context.

An example of where classroom observation affects the behaviour of teachers and pupils is the non-participant observation used in Ofsted. Whenever an inspector comes into a classroom to observe, everyone's behaviour changes. This is called the Hawthorne Effect and it weakens the validity of the observation. It is usually a problem with overt observation, as people know that they are being observed. In fact it is very difficult to be a covert observer of a classroom, unless you are one of the students doing an observation without the teacher knowing what is going on. Interactionists like participant observation, both overt and covert, because they want to understand social meanings and they want valid, in-depth data. They argue that you have to experience the situation as if you were one of the participants. Therefore, they would not like non-participant observation and would not trust the findings of Ofsted.

In conclusion, classroom observation is really the only way that we can see processes happening and this is especially important for aspects of the hidden curriculum. However, this is an area where it would be necessary to use triangulation, as the hidden curriculum affects so many different aspects of schooling.

🖉 A brief but reasoned conclusion that does not simply repeat what has gone before.

🖉 **Overall, the essay is coherent and well structured. The studies are appropriate to the method and there is a balance between strengths** and limitations. The item is referred to and used; there is a theoretical rationale and the appropriate use of relevant concepts. It would be difficult to produce an essay like this in an exam situation, but you should try to include theory, concepts and studies relevant to the question. The candidate scores the full 20 marks.

Question 3

This question permits you to draw examples from any areas of sociology with which you are familiar.

(a) Explain what is meant by the term 'sampling frame'. (2 marks)
(b) Suggest two ethical issues associated with the use of covert observation. (4 marks)
(c) Suggest two reasons why sociologists find official statistics useful. (4 marks)
**(d) Examine some of the factors that influence a researcher's choice
of method.** (20 marks)

Total: 30 marks

Answer to question 3: grade C candidate

(a) This is like the electoral register.

> 🖉 The candidate has given an example rather than a definition, but it is a correct example and scores 1 mark out of 2.

(b) Because the people know they are being observed the Hawthorne effect happens.

The researcher may be putting him/herself in danger.

Deception.

> 🖉 The candidate's first issue is incorrect, as 'covert' is confused with 'overt'. The second issue is a practical one not an ethical one and only the third is correct. The answer therefore scores 2 out of 4 marks.

(c) Time and money.

Because there is a large dark figure.

> 🖉 The candidate does not gain any marks here. Time and money could be made relevant by qualifying them, as in 'saves time and money'. It is not clear what is meant by the second reason.

(d) Many factors can influence a sociologist's choice of method. This can depend on what the researcher is investigating and using the most suitable method to do so. An example would be Durkheim in his famous work on suicide. Durkheim used the comparative method.

📝 Although the candidate refers to 'many factors', there is little development of this point. The example is descriptive and doesn't explain why Durkheim used this method.

Sociologists choose methods based on what kind of sociologist they are. For example, a functionalist or feminist would probably use different methods. Functionalists are linked with positivism and feminists are linked with interpretivist methods. Functionalists look on society as a 'real' thing and want to get quantitative data like official statistics.

📝 Again, the points are stated rather than explained and developed.

Interpretivists, on the other hand, look on society through the eyes of the people within that society. They like qualitative data because it is more in-depth and more valid. With secondary data they use content analysis and look for themes and meanings in diaries, letters and TV programmes.

📝 There is some reasonable development here and the candidate has started to focus on the factors influencing choice of method.

Another factor that can affect choice is time. If they want to carry out a study over a long time they would choose the longitudinal survey. They may use the snowball sampling method here to get people for the research. Sociologists who wish to look at one particular group may use a case study, which is good for accuracy. They could also use the comparative method to look at people from different places.

📝 There are practical factors behind choice here, but the points are simply stated. Reference to specific studies might be helpful, as the candidate could explain why a given sociologist had chosen a specific method or methods.

It is possible to use experiments but not very often as they are artificial. This is why the field experiment is used.

📝 **The essay comes to an abrupt end without a reasoned conclusion, thus losing some valuable points for evaluation. The candidate is awarded 12 out of 20 marks.**

Answer to question 3: grade-A candidate

(a) A sampling frame is a list of names or addresses of the target population that the researcher chooses the sample from. It can be a school register or a doctor's list of patients.

📝 This is a sound definition and includes appropriate examples as well. It would gain 2 marks for the definition alone, but it is often a good idea to use an example to illustrate the definition.

(b) Lack of informed consent.

Researcher may have to conduct illegal activities.

Putting the lives of others at risk.

There are three correct issues here and any two would score. It is useful in these short-answer questions to add a third possibility just in case one of the others is considered incorrect. The answer gains the full 4 marks.

(c) Positivists argue that they are both valid and reliable.

Positivists believe that they are objective hard data.

They are representative.

The candidate has produced four possible correct reasons here. Validity has been qualified by linking it to positivists. Four out of 4 marks.

(d) There are three main factors that influence a researcher's choice of method. These are practical, ethical and theoretical. Some researchers argue that the most important of these three is theoretical, as the method chosen by the researcher is usually based on their attitudes to science.

This is a sound introduction. The candidate has referred to the P, E and T factors and already made an evaluative point.

There are many practical factors that have to be taken into account, such as time, cost, access, opportunity and danger. Perhaps the most important is cost, because this affects a lot of things. If you have enough money you can have a large-scale survey research, use many interviewers and other people to collate the data. With little money, you might have to work alone and use participant observation.

The candidate is focused on the question, linking factors to choice of method. There is good application and analysis. It is important not to confuse methods with topic of research here.

Who funds the research is also very important. Government bodies may take ownership of the findings and not allow them to be published. Funding bodies may dictate the methods and this may go against the approach of the researcher. Project Camelot is an example of research that was funded by the Pentagon and the aims weren't known to the researchers. When they found out, many left the project.

This is an important paragraph. Candidates often fail to refer to funding bodies and these may well be the key influence on choice of research methods. The candidate has also implicitly referred to ethical factors here.

Generally, functionalists and Marxists use positivistic approaches, as they believe that social reality is capable of being observed and measured. This means that they use methods that produce quantitative, reliable data. They look for cause and effect relationships, so they compare social facts and investigate trends and patterns in social behaviour. For secondary data they prefer official statistics, like Durkheim's use of suicide statistics in different European countries in the nineteenth century. They see reliability and representativeness as very important, because they want to generalise and make predictions.

However, interpretivists follow Weber, who argued that sociologists should look for meanings of social action and use *verstehen* in their work. They prefer qualitative methods, especially those that allow the respondent to talk for themselves — like unstructured interviews and participant observation, where the researcher can become one of the group and see interactions taking place. This is why they look for validity in the research.

🖉 These two paragraphs focus on the theoretical context of methods. Sound links are made between sociological perspective and choice of method. The candidate also uses relevant concepts appropriately.

Laud Humphreys in *Tearoom Trade* used covert participant observation when he took the role of 'watch queen'. He was able to look at the men's interactions without actually taking part himself, but this produced some ethical problems, as participants weren't aware that Humphreys was researching them.

🖉 This is a relevant study well applied.

James Patrick also went undercover, in a Glasgow gang. He could not have done this research using methods like questionnaires or structured interviews, as the boys in the gang would not have answered questions on their deviant behaviour. But again, he deceived the gang and he became involved in deviant behaviour. Ethical considerations often cause researchers to use overt observation.

🖉 Another relevant and applied study.

Some feminist researchers argue that it is important to make a relationship with the people being researched. This is the case with Anne Oakley in *From Here to Maternity*, when she told the pregnant women that she was a researcher. In her study, she helped the women to get information from the hospital, so she was able to give something back to them in return for her researching them. So there are many factors that affect the choice of method. It is difficult to say which are the most important, but funding is certainly very significant.

🖉 This is another well-applied and relevant study. There is also a short conclusion that tries to evaluate the importance of factors affecting choice.

🖉 **Overall, this is a sophisticated, competent and coherent (but lengthy) essay. It is unlikely that many candidates could reproduce this under exam conditions. However, it would be possible to produce a shorter version and still gain top band marks, as long as the relevant skills were demonstrated. This answer earns 20 out of 20 marks.**

Paper 3

Total for this paper: 90 marks

Question 1

Read Item A below and answer parts (a) to (d) that follow.

Item A

It is argued that some teachers can make a difference to whether a student is successful in education or not. There is a great deal of sociological evidence to show that if teachers demonstrate negative attitudes towards some students this can affect the self-esteem and educational progress of those students. This labelling process, where it is successful, can result in a self-fulfilling prophecy. Some of these labels are based on the teachers' values and attitudes to social class. Some students who are seen as having more cultural capital than others are likely to be treated more positively by their teachers.

(a) Explain what is meant by the term 'cultural capital'. (2 marks)
(b) Suggest *three* ways in which schooling may be seen to be ethnocentric. (6 marks)
(c) Outline some of the ways in which schooling mirrors the world of work. (12 marks)
(d) Using material from Item A and elsewhere, assess the view that labelling is the major cause of pupils' underachievement. (20 marks)

Total: 40 marks

Answer to question 1: grade C candidate

(a) This is where middle-class pupils do better at school because they have more money to buy computers.

> The candidate confuses cultural with material capital and does not score any marks.

(b) This is where white is seen as better. It happens in the way subjects like history are taught.

> Although the candidate is aware of the concept, there are no specific ways shown. The reference to history, unfortunately, does not elaborate on how it may be ethnocentric. Note also that only two suggestions are offered, not the three that were asked for. Always read the question carefully and make sure that you do what the question asks. This answer does not score any marks.

(c) Willis said that school teaches working-class kids how to get working-class jobs. He studied two groups of working-class boys, one called 'the lads' and the other called 'the ear'oles'. The lads spent their time at school having a 'laff' and messed around. They hated the ear'oles because those boys were hard working and wanted good skilled jobs. The lads thought that school was really boring and messed around to make the teachers angry. They left school without any qualifications and so went into dead-end jobs. When they were in work Willis said that they were still messing around but the system needed workers in dead-end jobs.

🖉 The candidate has shown some reasonable knowledge and understanding appropriate to the question but the answer is not as well focused as it might be. It only offers one implicit way (cultural reproduction) in which schooling mirrors the world of work. There is very limited analysis/evaluation. The answer gains 5 out of 12 marks.

(d) Labelling means that teachers treat some students differently from others. They may label them 'lazy', 'troublemaker' and 'clown'. This could cause a self-fulfilling prophecy. This means that the label sticks and they fail.

🖉 This is a reasonable start. The candidate demonstrates a reasonable knowledge and understanding of the process of labelling and the self-fulfilling prophecy.

Hargreaves' study showed that teachers make judgements about pupils from the beginning. They call pupils lazy, good, bad, troublesome etc. These labels affect a pupil because if he or she is labelled as a troublemaker this will affect their feelings about themselves and about how they see school. He also said that setting and streaming were bad for students, because if you are in the bottom set then you will feel like a failure and the teachers will treat you differently. Then you are likely to give up and fail. The television programme *The Eye of the Storm* showed that when the teacher put collars on the pupils and treated them differently because of the colour of their eyes, their test results went down. Interactionists believe that people live up to their labels, which are a self-fulfilling prophecy, and some labels are harder to get rid of than others.

🖉 This paragraph starts well with appropriate sociological evidence. The reference to the television programme is rather simplistic and does not draw out the implications of the experiment in sufficient detail. The candidate makes useful reference to other in-school processes. There is some repetition at the end of this paragraph.

Ray Rist's study of the tigers, cardinals and clowns showed that 'What teachers believe, their students achieve'. Rist said that the teacher's labelling of the children was based on appearance and behaviour. Rist went back at the end of a year and the children were still in the same groups. This shows that labelling sticks. So labelling is very important in the success of pupils, but home factors are important too.

In conclusion, sociologists believe that many students fail, especially black boys, due to teachers' labelling.

🖉 **Overall, a reasonable attempt at the question. The candidate demonstrates sound knowledge and understanding of the labelling process and some studies. It is mainly descriptive and there is very limited evaluation and analysis. It gains 12 out of 20 marks.**

Answer to question 1: grade A candidate

(a) Middle-class pupils do better at school because they have the right attitudes and values from their parents. Parents know more about the education system and can work it to their advantage, like paying for private tuition for their children.

> Although the example given isn't strictly cultural capital, as it refers to economic capital, the candidate's response is sufficient to score the full 2 marks.

(b) Where schooling is ethnocentric it is biased towards white culture. History may only refer to black experience in terms of slavery. Literature would be European/white and religion would be based on Christianity. There may be tokenism as well, where festivals are celebrated once a year. This has sometimes been referred to as 'saris, samosas and steel drums'.

> This response is full and has more than three ways that schooling may be seen as ethnocentric. The candidate clearly understands the concepts so gains 6 out of 6 marks.

(c) Sociologists argue that there are many ways that schooling mirrors the world of work. Functionalists say that schooling prepares individuals for work to make them into efficient workers. This is for the benefit of society. However, Marxists say that schooling is really for the benefit of the capitalist system and pupils are taught to become obedient workers at school.

Bowles and Gintis argued that the economy cast a long shadow over school. They say school operates to the correspondence principle. This means that schools really work to meet the needs of capitalists. B & G say pupils learn lots of different subjects at school and the day is broken up into these subjects so that students have no control over their day or how they learn. B & G compare this to the experience of work, in which workers are disempowered.

Through the hidden curriculum pupils learn the values of capitalist society. For example, they learn to be obedient to authority, to be disciplined, to put up with boredom and to compete with others. B & G say that this prepares them to be docile workers. However, from an interpretivist's perspective, this does not take into account the reality of school life. Pupils do not necessarily accept what teachers say and many actively resist and rebel.

> This response is well focused on the question. There is good knowledge and understanding of sociological arguments and the candidate demonstrates explicit analysis and evaluation. It scores the full 12 marks.

(d) Some sociologists such as interactionists argue that processes inside schools, especially labelling, play an important role in a pupil's success or failure in education. Because interactionists focus on interactions between individuals, they are especially interested in the relationship between teachers and students.

> This is a sound start. It is well focused and provides the theoretical context to labelling.

One of the most important studies into labelling is Rosenthal and Jacobson's. They claimed to teachers that they had a test that could identify 'spurters' (children who would do well). In fact, they had randomly selected 20% of the pupils in the school. They told the teachers the test 'results' and came back a year later. They then gave the children another test and compared the results with the first test. They found that the 'spurters' had generally scored more highly than the rest. R & J argued that this was due to teacher expectations. Although their study has been criticised for ethical and methodological problems with their research, they showed how the self-fulfilling prophecy took place.

e This candidate demonstrates accurate knowledge and understanding, well applied to the question.

Another important study of labelling is Rist's research of a kindergarten class. By the end of their first week at nursery, the teacher had placed the 5-year-olds on three separate tables named the tigers, cardinals and clowns. Rist argued that pupils were labelled on the basis of appearance and how they spoke rather than their abilities. The seating did not change for the rest of the year but the tigers did much better than the other groups. Rist concluded that 'what teachers believe, their pupils achieve'.

Gillborn also said that Afro-Caribbean students were more likely to receive negative labels from staff. Teachers tended to stereotype the boys as unruly and disrespectful. The boys were seen as more challenging and difficult to control and they were dealt with more harshly than other boys were. The Afro-Caribbean boys saw this as unfair and as a result lived up to the negative stereotype.

However, not all interactionists accept this deterministic view of labelling. Margaret Fuller's research on black girls showed that they were able to resist the labels of their teachers and achieve despite them. Mac an Ghaill also showed the process to be more complex, where students often ignored those staff they felt were being racist towards them.

e These paragraphs provide excellent evidence to support the argument. There is conceptually detailed knowledge and understanding together with explicit analysis and evaluation.

In conclusion, it is clear that labelling plays a very important role in students' achievement. However, it is important to say that other factors, such as home background, poverty and health will also play a part in this process. So we cannot say that labelling is the main factor.

e This conclusion introduces us to the other factors that have a part to play in educational success and is evaluative.

e **The candidate provides a thorough response with a clear and coherent structure leading to a reasoned conclusion. Appropriate sociological evidence is applied to the question and the answer gains 20 out of 20 marks.**

paper

Question 2

This question requires you to apply your knowledge and understanding of socio-logical research methods to the study of this particular issue in education.

Read Item B and answer the question that follows.

Item B

The interactionist perspective suggests that not all children respond to schooling in the same way. Individual children attach different meanings to school and relate in different ways to the school experience. Often, teachers treat some groups of children differently from others, and attach negative labels to them. In some cases the response to this differential treatment from teachers results in resistance and even the development of anti-school subcultures. When conducting research into schooling, interactionists prefer methods that produce qualitative data, such as participant observation and unstructured interviews.

Using material from Item B and elsewhere, assess the strengths and limitations of one of the following methods for the study of pupil subcultures:

(i) Questionnaires
(ii) Participant observation   **20 marks**

Answer to question 2: grade C candidate

(ii) In order to study pupil subcultures at first hand, many sociologists would choose parti-cipant observation (PO) as their method. There are two types of PO, covert and overt. Covert means that the observer is hidden, but in overt the observer tells the subjects what they are doing in the research. Paul Willis used PO to study working-class lads in school. He was overt because he was too old to pretend to be a student. He studied 12 boys called the 'lads'. Another group of boys were called the 'ear'oles' because they listened to the teachers and they wanted to get qualifications for jobs later on. However, the lads were different. They liked to mess around and 'have a laff'.

> 🖉 A reasonable start. The candidate has identified two types of PO and given an example. It is important to note that the candidate has already given more description of the study than is necessary for this question.

According to Item B, interactionists say that not all pupils are treated in the same way by their teachers and this may result in subcultures. Hargreaves showed that setting and streaming caused pupil subcultures. Children in lower sets have lower self-esteem and start to hate school because they feel themselves to be failures. This makes them turn against school and reject its values. Therefore, to stop subcultures developing we should not set or stream in schools.

e This paragraph could have been made relevant if the candidate had focused on the methods that Hargreaves used, not the findings. The question asks for strengths and limitations of PO and as yet, the candidate has failed to address this issue.

Interactionists see PO as a valid method because you can get very close to the truth. Willis could not have gained the same information if he had given the lads a questionnaire to fill in. People often lie on questionnaires and the lads would not have taken them seriously.

e This paragraph is more focused and the candidate attempts some contrast evaluation by using problems of questionnaires.

However, positivists see PO as unethical and biased. It is unreliable and not representative.

e The candidate comes to an abrupt end. It is always worthwhile to write a conclusion in order to gain more marks for evaluation.

e **Although much of this response is tangential to the question, the candidate does focus at times and gains marks for this, earning 10 out of 20 marks.**

Answer to question 2: grade A candidate

(i) At first sight questionnaires are not the most obvious choice of research method for the topic of pupil subcultures. However, sometimes the funding body insists that a quantitative method should be used, despite the researcher's preferences.

e This is a sophisticated introduction to the essay. The candidate is using his/her sociological imagination. This would be a highly unusual response, but already the candidate has grabbed the attention of the reader.

Questionnaires are simply pre-set schedules of questions which are given to all respondents in exactly the same way. This makes the method highly reliable and is favoured by positivists because they are considered to be both objective and valid. Questionnaires allow researchers to gain a much larger response from a wider sample than, for example, unstructured interviews. However, according to Item B, interactionists would prefer more qualitative methods to gain a more in-depth understanding and insight.

e The candidate demonstrates excellent knowledge and understanding of the chosen method and its advantages. The method is located theoretically and evaluated. However, as yet the candidate has not linked the method to pupil subcultures.

Not many sociologists would use a questionnaire to gain information on subcultures. By their very nature, subcultures are not accessible. Willis managed to get his information by being with the lads, listening and gaining their trust by talking to them. Interactionists would dismiss questionnaire data as invalid. For example, Labov's work showed that qualitative methods were more appropriate for researching children.

e Again a concise, coherent paragraph. The candidate refers to two appropriate studies, but does not fall into the trap of describing the findings.

Interactionists would argue that we cannot come close to social reality by simply imposing the researcher's constructs on the people being studied. Questionnaire design is said to reflect the values of the researcher. Even for positivists, question-naires would be considered more useful for collecting factual data, such as social class, qualifications, attitudes to school and parental background, than under-standing subcultures.

e The candidate demonstrates a sophisticated understanding of methodology. It is impressive to see that he/she refers to an in-house criticism of positivists.

In conclusion, it is clear that questionnaires are not the most appropriate method to gain an understanding of the reality of school subcultures. They may produce a lot of data but they do not capture the social reality of those involved because, as Weber said, sociologists need to use *verstehen*.

e **An extremely sophisticated, conceptually detailed and well-structured response that will gain full marks, 20 out of 20. It is important to note that it is possible to gain full marks with a less sophisticated answer.**

Question 3

This question permits you to draw examples from any areas of sociology with which you are familiar.

(a) Explain what is meant by the term 'sampling unit'. (2 marks)
(b) Suggest two types of sampling technique. (4 marks)
(c) Suggest two reasons why some sociologists choose to collect qualitative data. (4 marks)
(d) Examine the problems sociologists may face in using different kinds of secondary data in their research. (20 marks)

Total: 30 marks

Answer to question 3: grade C candidate

(a) As on the electoral register = one person on the list.

e The candidate has given an example rather than a definition, but it is a correct one and scores 1 mark out of a possible 2.

(b) Snowball sampling

Random sampling

e Two correct techniques given, earning 4 out of 4 marks.

(c) More valued

They want *verstehen*

More truthful data

> 🖉 'More valued' does not score but there are two other appropriate reasons here, so 4 out of 4 marks awarded.

(d) Secondary data are used by all kinds of sociologists. Positivists use them because they give quantitative data and interpretivists use them to get qualitative data. Secondary data come from historical documents, diaries, letters, official statistics and so on.

> 🖉 The paragraph introduces the concept and gives appropriate examples. Theoretical location is present, but not developed.

Laslett did a survey on the family — he wanted to know how the size of the family changed over time and he used secondary sources like parish records. This was good because it was a survey of the past and all the people were dead. However, there are problems because Laslett couldn't really test how true the records were. They were usually collected by clergymen who might not have taken accurate data. Also, some of the births may not have been recorded, as they were illegitimate.

> 🖉 This is a relevant study and has some appropriate evaluation but lacks major concepts. There is focus on problems of the data.

Anne Frank's diary is valid because she wrote down her experiences at the time, but it isn't representative, because she was a middle-class girl and she wouldn't have known what it was like for working-class families. It's not reliable either because we only have one diary.

> 🖉 Again, this is a useful example with evaluation and relevant concepts.

Positivists like official statistics because they say that they are valid and reliable, but interpretivists wouldn't agree. Positivists say that as the government produces them, we can trust them and sociologists wouldn't be able to do without these figures. Interpretivists argue that they are sometimes made up by governments to look good, like crime and unemployment statistics, and even league tables have problems.

So we can see there are problems with these data. Overall there are more benefits than problems as they are free or cheap and available and some are in statistical tables.

> 🖉 There is contrast here between the major perspectives, but the inclusion of examples to illustrate the problems of official statistics would be rewarded.

> 🖉 **Overall, there is useful knowledge and understanding, but the focus is not always clear. The candidate has produced a 'uses versus limitations' response rather than one focused on problems. However, there are several points raised and the candidate refers to theory, some concepts, one appropriate study and one example, so gains 12 out of 20 marks.**

paper

Answer to question 3: grade A candidate

(a) A sampling unit is one person/household/business etc. from a sampling frame. It coud be one pupil on the school register.

> This is a sound definition and includes an appropriate example as well. It would gain 2 marks for the definition alone, but it is often a good idea to use an example to illustrate the definition.

(b) Quota sampling

Stratified random sampling

Non-representative (the affluent worker)

> Any two from the three listed would score 4 out of 4 marks.

(c) Interpretivists prefer this type of data as it is more meaningful, more in-depth and gives insight.

> 'Interpretivists prefer it' would not score, as it is not a reason. However, the candidate has also given three other appropriate reasons and any two would count, so it gains 4 out of 4 marks.

(d) Secondary data are collected by another researcher for another purpose. Using secondary data, such as historical documents and diaries and letters of the time, may be the only way to examine the past, but we have to be very careful in terms of validity and reliability. Although there are many advantages to using secondary data (like cost-effectiveness, as they are often free or cheap, easy to get hold of, cover the past and in many different types), we are going to look at the problems with them.

> A good introduction that demonstrates knowledge and understanding and is already focused on problems.

Personal documents will not be reliable as they are mainly one-offs, like a letter or a diary of one individual. They could be fakes, like Hitler's diaries, or they could be someone's fantasy of what their lives were really like. A politician's diary is likely to show the best side of the person, rather than revealing that they had been involved in any corruption.

> There is a selection of possible problems here, but little analysis.

Even though these data may save time from not having to do the research, you still have to go through loads of documents to find anything that's relevant to the present research.

There aren't so many ethical problems compared with some primary data, but sometimes you may be using personal documents without the individual's permission, even if another member of the family gave you the permission.

e There are both practical and ethical criticisms here; the latter are often ignored in a question like this.

Theoretically, all researchers can use secondary data, but there are problems. Positivists use official statistics because they say that they are social facts, but interpretivists argue that there's the 'dark figure' with soft statistics such as crime and unemployment. Durkheim used suicide statistics in his study, but he assumed that the figures were correct and later researchers have criticised him for not treating them as socially constructed. But without statistics it would have been impossible for Durkheim to go around collecting all the data for himself. Official statistics are also open to the accusation of manipulation, as past governments have massaged the figures to make themselves look good, or changed definitions such as eligibility for unemployment to reduce the overall figures.

e This is a very good paragraph. The reference to 'soft' statistics is sound and the candidate has developed the argument well.

We know that criminal statistics are those reported and recorded. With rape, for example, only about 5% of people accused of rape get convicted. Feminists show that many victims are afraid to tell the police and the majority of rapists go free.

Marxists say that official statistics are not to be trusted because they reinforce the ideology of the ruling class, by focusing on the crimes of the working class rather than corporate and white-collar crimes.

e These are two important criticisms and each is well developed.

Although there are many problems with secondary data, John Scott said they are useful as long as we take into account their authenticity (are they what they say they are?), their credibility (can we believe them?), their representativeness (can we use them to generalise?), and their meaning (can we be sure we know what they mean?).

e A rather abrupt conclusion, but again with an evaluative tone.

e **Overall, the essay is well focused on the question. Although slightly lacking in sociological studies, there are some practical and ethical problems and sound theoretical argument and this answer gains 18 out of 20 marks.**

This is a question for you to attempt yourself. We have given you some tips for each of the sections.

Total for this paper: 90 marks

Question 1

Read Item A below and answer parts (a) to (d) that follow.

> **Item A**
>
> A number of recent government policies have been introduced in order to make the education system more market-orientated. These policies include parental choice, league tables and changes in funding arrangements. Some sociologists have argued that the effect of these policies has been to produce a more unequal educational system.
>
> Changes in the relationship between schools and parents have been especially significant for middle-class parents. It is argued that as the power of the local education authorities has declined, middle-class parents have been able to exploit the situation in the interests of their own children. Although working-class parents might be as interested as middle-class parents in their children's schooling, they tend not to have the knowledge and skills to influence decisions over which schools their children attend. Consequently, middle-class students fill the more desirable and usually more successful schools.

(a) Explain what is meant by the term 'ethnocentric' curriculum. (2 marks)

> **Tip** It is a good idea to give the definition and add an example, such as 'Literature will only be the study of white British or European authors'. If your definition is incorrect, you might still score 1 mark for a correct example.

(b) Suggest *three* material factors that may be responsible for working-class underachievement at school. (6 marks)

> **Tip** Watch here that you are giving material factors and don't confuse them with cultural factors such as parental values. Material factors relate to economic issues, such as poverty and poor housing. Try to think of three factors in addition to those suggested here.

(c) Outline some of the reasons why females now achieve higher results than males in the education system. (12 marks)

> **Tip** Here you must concentrate on the reasons why girls are achieving, not on reasons why boys are not doing so well. Remember, 'the education system' includes colleges and universities as well as schools.

(d) Using material from Item A and elsewhere, assess the view that the marketisation of education has created greater inequality in education. (20 marks)

> **Tip** It is good practice when reading the item to underline the aspects that will be relevant to this essay. Make sure that you refer to the item and, better still, use relevant concepts and phrases from it in your answer.

If you are not familiar with market orientation, refer back to the sections on policies in education. You will find the section on the 1988 Education Act and more recent Labour government policies helpful. As this question asks you to *assess* the view, you will need to produce more than one argument. It is not enough simply to agree with the proposed viewpoint. Can you think of some evidence that would suggest that some of the policies have benefited working-class pupils as well as middle-class ones? This question tests your skills of analysis and evaluation. The assessment skills here are AO1 = 8 and AO2 = 12, so it is important that you interpret the question, apply appropriate material, analyse and evaluate the material to gain as many marks as you can.

Total: 40 marks

Question 2

This question requires you to apply your knowledge and understanding of sociological research methods to the study of **this particular issue** in education.

Read Item B and answer the question that follows

Item B

Since research began into educational achievement, many social commentators have argued that social class has played the most significant role in the differences in students' achievement. Even though various governments have attempted to create equality through their policies, social class continues to advantage some students and to disadvantage others. In fact some sociologists, such as Professor Diane Reay, maintain that the educational attainment gap between the classes was as great in 2007 as it was 50 or 100 years ago. She sees remarkably little progress having been made over the last 100 years towards social justice and equality in education for the working classes.

Using material from Item B and elsewhere, assess the strengths and limitations of one of the following methods for the study of the effects of social-class background on pupil achievement:

(i) Case study

(ii) Social surveys **20 marks**

Tip Read Item B carefully and note down what you know about social class background and educational achievement. (It might be helpful to re-read the sections in this book that refer to differential achievement and social class.)

Think about the two methods and how appropriate each would be. Choose the one that for you would produce the more appropriate data to answer the question.

Always make reference to and use the material in the item, as you are not really addressing the question unless you do this.

You must assess the *usefulness* of your chosen method, so that means its strengths and limitations. A useful way of being evaluative is to contrast your chosen method with others. So you might argue that the case study allows the researcher to use a variety of methods to study this topic, unlike using a single method such as, say, structured interviews, which would only allow you to collect quantitative data. Keep your focus on the issue of social class and achievement; you will also be rewarded if you refer to studies that have examined this particular issue.

With any question that asks you to assess usefulness, think practical, ethical and theoretical (PET) factors. This will help you to get top band marks.
AO1 skills = 8 and AO2 skills = 12

Question 3

This question permits you to draw examples from any areas of sociology with which you are familiar.

(a) Explain what is meant by the term 'hypothesis'. (2 marks)

Tip Do not forget to bring in the idea of 'testing' a statement.

(b) Suggest one advantage and one disadvantage of the longitudinal survey as a research method. (4 marks)

Tip Make sure that you are clear what a longitudinal survey is (a study conducted at intervals over a long period of time, usually with the same sample).

(c) Suggest two reasons why interpretivist sociologists reject the use of official statistics. (4 marks)

Tip Be clear that you refer to interpretivists specifically. You could look at reasons such as invalid data and the lack of social meanings. Make sure that you focus on official statistics, not simply quantitative data.

(d) Examine the reasons why sociologists rarely use the laboratory method in research. (20 marks)

Tip This is a less commonly asked question than those about other methods, as sociology tends to reject the laboratory method in favour of other methods such as the comparative method or the use of social surveys. However, it is an important question and one that you might be faced with. It is vital that you look at 'reasons' why it is rarely used, rather than the strengths and limitations of the method.

It is again important to structure the response in terms of practical, ethical and theoretical factors. Theoretically, it is important to look at the reasons why positivistic sociologists might justify the laboratory method, even though they might not choose to use it themselves. It has been a method traditionally favoured by psychologists, and sociologists have sometimes made use of their work. Studies that you might refer to are those of Milgram, Bandura and Zimbardo. Again, you are examining these studies in order to show why sociologists reject them; this allows you to engage the interpretivist critique.

Practical reasons might include artificiality and problems with sampling. Ethical factors are significant here, as the BSA guidelines oppose any research that might place subjects at risk of short-term or long-term effects. It helps to contrast the method with others that might be used to research the same topic, and you might look at the use of field experiments, which use the natural environment of the social actors.

AO1 skills = 10, AO2 = 10 so you need to balance knowledge and understanding with application, interpretation, analysis and evaluation.

Good luck!

Total: 30 marks